SKI TOURING IN SCOTLAND

Looking west to The Stuic. Easter 1988 on the White Mounth (Tour 23)

SKI TOURING IN SCOTLAND

BY

ANGELA OAKLEY

CICERONE PRESS
MILNTHORPE, CUMBRIA

ISBN 1 85284 054 4

For skiers,
whatever their age or ability,
who love and respect the landscape
they move through.

CONTENTS

LOCATION OF ROUTES, TOURS AND SKI AREAS

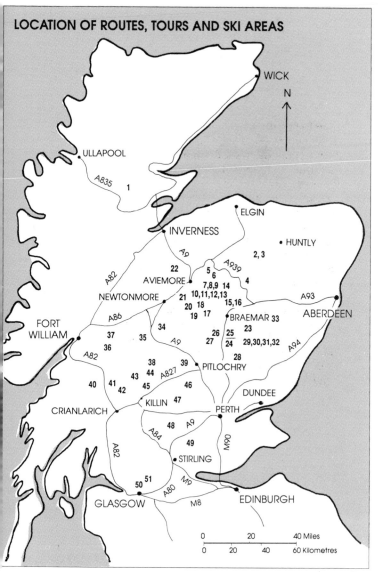

ACKNOWLEDGEMENTS

In collecting the information on snow cover and terrain given in this guide I have sought the local knowledge of many fellow skiers. I wish to thank them, for the information they have readily given has meant detailed accounts of snow cover over the seasons, and ski runs of quality could be indicated.

Much of the information has been given by skiers in the Nordic Ski Clubs of Scotland. The Inverness Nordic Ski Club provided details on Ben Wyvis, Tayside Nordic Ski Club supplied information on Mount Keen, Glen Clova and Glen Isla, Tom Mowat of Norscot was especially helpful in the research of Clashindarroch Forest. The staff at Highland Guides, Inverdruie contributed greatly to descriptions of ski runs in the Cairngorms, Monadhliath and Speyside forests. Information was also supplied by Malcolm Rawson, Brian Adams, Ann Wakeling and a host of other individuals.

Philip Oakley researched several areas on my behalf, bringing home excellent notes, when the births of our children interrupted my own hillgoings.

My thanks go to them all.

Angela Oakley

INTRODUCTION

The pleasures of ski touring in the Scottish countryside have been enjoyed by an increasing number of enthusiasts since the start of this century. After 1960 the growth of interest accelerated, accompanied by an increase in the desire to find the best places to ski. Among skiers a healthy exchange of information has established some facts about where the snow is likely to be found and which terrain gives the best ski running. This book aims to record some of this knowledge, and inform the skier of worthwhile ski areas, routes and runs.

The guide does not cover all areas of Scotland, nor all the ski routes within the areas chosen. There is much unrecorded for the explorer to seek out for himself. Indeed the surprise and satisfaction of discovering a ski run is part of the pleasure of ski touring, and the challenge of venturing into the unknown will thrill and awaken an adventurer to the needs of his surroundings so as to sharpen his wits and open his eyes to the snowscape around him.

As such the information imparted here serves as an introduction to ski routes in Scotland. Tours have been chosen because they give good skiing in a variety of landscapes. All abilities have been included.

This book should be used in conjunction with Ordnance Survey maps, which is where the ski tourer will find the main body of his information on a tour. The 1:50,000 Second Series maps are ideal for mountain and hill touring. Within forests the 1:25,000 maps are sometimes more helpful.

*   *   *

In general there are two criteria required for a ski route - snow cover and suitable terrain. The routes in this book have been chosen because they may have snow cover when other areas do not, and because the terrain is particularly suited to the kick and glide movements of the Nordic ski. Skiers using ski mountaineering gear will not always find these routes suitable for their equipment, or will prefer a different route to the same destination. Since most ski tourers travel by car to the start of a route, and only complete a day's skiing before returning to that vehicle, emphasis has been placed on circular tours of a few hours. The direction the circuit is skied will depend on wind direction on exposed sections, the quality or difficulty of descent, and the scenery to be faced. Since much of Scottish snow lies above the 650m contour line mountain tours are given generous attention. However it should be stressed that simply ascending and descending a peak to "bag" it reduces the joy of Nordic touring - that is travelling on skis across snowy expanses. Where possible mountain ascents are included as one part of a larger tour.

A ski tourer will often choose to ski in an area regarded by walkers as unattractive. Even if they choose the same area, their routes across it will be different. The rugged and jagged narrow ridges of the W coast with their steep gullies and chimneys are beautiful in winter, but not ski touring terrain. Yet the vast expanses of bog which are a nightmare to walkers, will give a sound skiing surface when snow-covered and the opportunity to kick and glide into remote and little-visited areas. The high level plateaux of the East where "peaks" are sometimes no more than high points in gently undulating expanses might be uninspiring to walkers. To skiers they give excellent terrain, over which to move is the attraction. Whereas a walker may make use of a track, the skier will reject its restriction and "play" the snow field either side of it, particularly in descent. The winter walker may try to avoid deep snow and head for the wind-blown crests of ridges. The skier will use the gently angled deeply filled and sheltered burns. For seasoned hill-walkers who take up ski touring as an extension to their outdoor activities it may take some re-thinking to plan a day's route.

Scotland has some excellent langlauf terrain. The problem is snow cover. Our temperate maritime climate means we suffer greatly at the expense of thaws or snowless periods. However, optimistically there is usually some skiable snow somewhere in Scotland every year and a possibility of skiing from October to June.

Snow cover depends on two factors - firstly snow falling and secondly snow holding.

Snowfall in Scotland

Snowfall in Scotland is affected primarily by the direction the winds crossing the country come from, and the relief of the land. The prevailing winds are south-westerlies. These carry large amounts of precipitation and so can give a snow fall to the mountains of the W.

However, they are warm winds, originating in warmer climates and heated by the Gulf Stream. If they persist they are more likely to bring mild rainy weather to the country, and meagre snow falls. When Britain is affected in winter by cold winds from the Arctic, snow will fall. These winds pick up water as they cross the northern seas, and are heavily laden. They are not frequent visitors, but when they do come they are capable of covering much of Scotland with snow within hours. It is common for winds to reach Britain from the E and NE when an anticyclone develops over Northern Europe. Air moves around the high pressure, zone reaching Britain after crossing the cold continental climatic zones of Europe, picking up water as it crosses the North Sea. These winds bring much snow to Eastern Scotland.

The consequences of these wind patterns mean that generally the E gets more snow than the W. The E is protected by mountains in the W from the thawing westerlies. The W is in the rain shadow of the snow-bearing easterlies. Close watching of wind patterns will indicate to the ski tourer where snow has been falling. It is essential to watch the pattern over the whole winter if knowledge of the snow cover is to be built up. One snowfall may cover the ground for many weeks.

Both W and E have upland areas. This affects snowfall, as temperature decreases with height and so dictates whether it is snow or rain that falls. Also uplift of air causes cooling and precipitation to occur in the first place. Conditions vary but a simple rule of a reduction in temperature of 2 to 3 degrees centigrade per 300m gives an acceptable measure of cooling with height. Thus a lowland temperature forecast of 8 degrees centigrade may well be giving snowfall on mountain tops. Snow will lie on the ground if it falls through air colder than 3 degrees centigrade. If air is slightly warmer than this snow may still fall, but will melt on reaching the ground. When air temperatures are near 0 degrees centigrade a small rise in altitude can be crucial. This range of temperature is very common in Scotland in winter. The impact for the ski tourer is obvious. If you want to tour extensively in Scotland, you need to go to the higher altitudes. Table 1 gives an indication of some of the high places in Scotland. Once again it is the E that has tracts of land lying continuously above 800m. The Cairngorms are the snowiest part of Britain.

TABLE 1
HIGH PLATEAUX AREAS

	Land (square kilometres) above					
	800m	900m		1000m	
Ben Nevis and Aonach Mor	17	5.5	(8.5)	3	(5.5)
Ben Macdui and Cairn Gorm☆	39	33	(33)	20	(20)
Braeriach and the Moine Mhor☆☆	71	24	(49)	14	(22)
Beinn a' Bhuird and Ben Avon	56	32	(35)	9	(18)
The White Mounth and Glas Maol	70	18	(31)	5	(11)
Creag Meagaidh	27	10	(12)	2.5	(3.5)
Monadhliath	43	1	(3)	0	(0)
East Drumochter Hills	24	2	(3)	0	(0)

☆   Does not include the area NE of The Saddle, height 807m,
     including Bynack More

☆☆ These two plateaux join at the Pools of Dee, height 815m

Figures in brackets give the total area above 900m or 1000m inside the
800m contour line.
The base figure is the largest single area above 900m or 1000m inside
the 800m contour line.

Snowfall in Scotland is quite different from snowfall in the Alps. It
does not fall in one steady fall, and it rarely floats down vertically.
Drifting is the norm. Sadly snow is sometimes blown off the mountain
to warmer glens, where it melts.

Snow Holding

Once the snow has fallen it is crucial that it lies until the skier can
reach it. Warm air is the most efficient means of removing snow.

Sunshine will melt a thin snow cover, but it is not effective on a deeper cover, since the snow reflects it. If the sun does melt the surface, this may well re-freeze overnight. The ski tourer should not be deterred by a blazing sun! Warm air can however strip a hillside. Rain is damaging. Warm, wet air is a characteristic of westerly winds. These are the ski tourer's main enemy. They can remove snow at a rate of 65mm depth a day. Consequently snow cover in the W of Scotland does not last as long as that in the E, and even in the Cairngorms the E summits resist thaw better than the W ones. The E has a much longer season for ski touring than the W.

The effect of altitude on snow holding is such that the average number of days per annum with snow lying on the ground is 50 to 100 in the Scottish Highlands, but only 10 to 20 days in the Scottish Lowlands. That is why most of the areas covered in this book lie above 300m.

The ski tourer will find it worthwhile to seek out those roads which will take him to a high start point, for example the A93 which climbs to over 650m above sea level at the Cairnwell Pass. He might also note how quickly a route gains height after leaving the road. A short, steep climb on foot may look off-putting from the start point, but may well lead within minutes to skiable snow at the higher level.

Snow that reaches the ground in Scotland is usually picked up again by the wind and re-distributed. The wind will drop its load of snow as it slows down in sheltered places. This has advantages as it results in massive accumulations of snow in some places which last well. Fortunately many of these sheltered spots are where skiers would like snow to be, for example on forest and mountain tracks and in gullies which provide long access routes to high ground. Unfortunately it means there is rarely a uniform snow cover for very long.

Since the prevailing winds are south-westerlies it is most common to find snow has been lifted from SW slopes and deposited on NE-facing slopes. In general snow is more likely to be found on slopes facing NW, NE and SE. However it is worth observing the wind patterns throughout the winter and to study the local wind patterns to known where to expect the snow to be.

It is quite common for ridges to be blown clear and the skier is forced to look for snow below the crests. Similarly the high plateaux may be stripped of snow, yet the burns and corries filled deeply.

Shallow depressions hold snow well. Deeply incised pockets suffer the attacks of wind eddies and are generally not as good. Slight hollows or change in slope angle on a mountainside are places where snow lingers after thaw elsewhere. Patches in these can be usefully linked to traverse a hillside, whilst snow residing in ribbons along burns allow ascent and descent of that same hillside. Snow will drift into the troughs of peat hags, along walls, forest edges, and into drainage ditches. Grassy terrain resists removal of snow by wind, as flakes become trapped between the blades of grass.

There are some places in Scotland where snow patches have remained throughout the summer. These are in the high, NE-facing corries of Ben Nevis and the Cairngorm mountains for example at Garbh Choire on Braeriach and Ciste Mhearad on Cairn Gorm. It is not uncommon to find quite extensive skiable tracts on mid-summer's day. Indeed snow may fall on high ground at any time during the year, although in summer frozen precipitation usually falls as hail. Nevertheless the main skiing season is considered to be from December to early May, with skiing possible in some years in November and even October. Table 2 shows a generalised Nordic skier's calendar. However conditions do vary considerably from year to year, decade to decade and even century to century. The seventeenth century has been termed the "Little Ice Age" due to the general harshness of winters then. This century has seen some very mild, snowless years, for example from 1920 to 1929, 1932/33 and 1938, but also some very snowy years, for example 1947, 1951 and 1963. 1947 was the most snowy winter of this century. Every day between 22 January and 17 March there was a snowfall somewhere in Britain. On 25 February 1947 someone cycled the length of frozen Loch Morlich, and the glens of the Cairngorms were not clear of snow until April. 1963 was actually a colder year than 1947, but the quantity of snow falling was not as great.

A year of plentiful snow can be followed by a year of little snow. Indeed on 2 December 1948 an amazingly high temperature of 18.3 degrees centigrade was recorded in the Highlands at Achnashellach. The ski tourer should expect some years when there will be little or no skiing at low levels. In 1989 all the official Nordic ski races were cancelled due to lack of snow, and it was not until late February that any worthwhile ski touring could be undertaken.

It has been said that ski touring is not a winter but a spring sport.

TABLE 2 - GENERALISED NORDIC SKIING CALENDAR FOR SCOTLAND

October	November	December	January	February	March	April	May	June
Usually some skiing possible somewhere in Scotland →								
Always the chance of a snowfall, even at low levels. However any snow cover is likely to be short-lived, so take advantage of it quickly. ← →		Variable. White Christmases are not common, but there can be good quality snow in December ←	Usually Jan. before any permanent snow builds up.			Snow compacting in hollows and burns.	Snow cover patchy ← →	
			Main period of snowfall and best chances of snow at low levels. Snow building up in hollows, burns and depressions.				Snow line recedes ← →	
		Short daylight hours ← →					Evening skiing possible ← →	
		Strong winds, blizzards, storms ← →				Weather more settled, warm sunshine ← →		
Best chances on grassy, smooth and boulder-free terrain. Avoid long heather. ← →			Good chance of forest skiing ← →					
			Racing season ← →			High plateau and mountain touring at its best. Long runs in compacted gullies. ← →		Skiing restricted to a few remaining runs on high-level N-facing slopes.
Reasonable chance of snow at low levels - but this also means roads may be difficult - even blocked. However local skiing or short distances to the snow a possibility. ← →						Expect to drive long distances and then walk to the snow ← →		

15

Certainly there can be more skiable snow lying on 1 June than on 1 January, and Easter is better than Christmas for both snow cover and weather.

Terrain

Given snow cover and the necessary skiing ability much of Scotland is skiable. However certain terrain is particularly suited to Nordic skis. This is not always the sort of terrain best suited to hill walkers or skiers using ski mountaineering gear. The joy of Nordic touring is to travel by kick and glide movements across a snowscape. In general the Nordic tourer seeks broad slopes of easy gradient, although there are times when he prefers the challenge of a restricted steep descent. Modern equipment and advancement in thinking has meant that telemark skiers do ski some of the steepest runs at the downhill resorts.

At low levels forests give ideal skiing. Forest roads hold snow and are usually well-graded, often sandy and skiable with minimum cover. All the official Scottish cross-country ski races are currently held in forests. Disused railway tracks give easy level skiing. Golf courses and parks allow skiing in open spaces on a variety of slopes and have a short grass base which holds the snow between blades and is kind to ski soles.

At higher levels extensive undulating tracts of moorland and plateau give freedom to Nordic fluency. Table 1 lists some of these high level areas and indicates the degree to which they undulate, and thus their suitability for Nordic skis. In many places such plateau fall away steeply, and ways to reach and descend from the ski touring tablelands restrict the routes across them. Some are elongated, allowing one or two obvious routes. Others are compact giving a variety of routes across them. It is interesting to note that the highest areas do not always allow the longest routes across them. The Monadhliath, with 40 square kms undulating between the 800m and the 900m contour line appears favourable compared to the Ben Macdui and Cairn Gorm Plateau with only 6 square kms between the 800 and 900m contour line and 13 square kms between the 900m and the 1000m contour line. The White Mounth and Glas Maol Plateau has 59 square kms of land undulating between the 800m and 1000m contour lines. Since there are many accessible, scenic and easy approaches to this plateau it must be one of the most suitable areas in the country for Nordic ski touring.

*   *   *

Conditions the Skier will Encounter

1. *Weather*

It is usual to be accompanied by the wind. The direction will affect which way a tour is skied. It may also determine the route of the day, forcing a skier into sheltered corries or even into forests. At worst it will whip the snow into spindrift. It is worth finding out the predicted speed and direction of winds when route planning.

Above 600m poor visibility is common. In conditions of white out and wind it can be difficult on skis to perceive whether one is moving or stationary. Navigation becomes extremely difficult. Total white out is best avoided and routes at lower levels sought. Routes in light mist can be simplified by choosing areas with many reference points, such as those with lines of fence posts to follow. At lower levels skiing in the rain may have to be tolerated.

Occasionally there are conditions of calm, brilliant clarity and warm sunshine. The occurrence of these days ensures that the skier returns to tolerate the less favourable days. Even in Scotland the sun may be strong enough to cause harmful sunburn and headaches. Protection for the skin and eyes is necessary.

2. *Snow Conditions*

Deep powder is rare in Scotland. Expect a mix of ice, wind slab, heather and rock. Usually the snow has been molested by the wind and then tortured by the freeze thaw action of temperatures fluctuating around 0 degrees centigrade. It may have been fluted by the wind into sastrugi, small ridges separated by hollows, which disrupt ski running. Redistribution by the wind means wind slab is common. This can load a slope so that it becomes avalanche prone and therefore not the best route, even if it has the best snow cover. Breakable crust and wet snow resembling porridge can slow a skier down. It may be necessary to change waxes more than once as one ascends the different temperature bands between start point and summit. Total ground cover is not always present, and detours to connect snow patches, or a mix of walking and skiing may be required. Route planning needs to allow time for these inconveniences. Note also the occurrence of ice on forest and valley trails which may indicate that steel edged skis be preferable to light touring gear!

Spring snow can be very good in Scotland. This snow has suffered much freeze thaw action and resembles granular sugar. It is wet by day and may freeze overnight, in which case it is not pleasant. It is heavy but can give excellent running. It is worth building up knowledge of the snow over the whole winter to know what to expect in the spring.

Avalanches have killed Nordic skiers in Scotland. To date the numbers of both fatalities and injuries caused by avalanche among skiers in Scotland is small. However Nordic skiers are venturing onto steeper slopes than they have tended to do in the past. There is now a volume of information readily available on avalanche safety. It is worthwhile learning about snow slopes and incorporating this knowledge into route choice.

Ski Tourers' Responsibilities

Traditionally in Scotland there is a freedom to roam where we wish in the countryside. This is a tremendous luxury compared with the state of affairs in other countries. There are parts of the world where the awful situation is that skiers are controlled, must pay to ski and are banned from certain areas. The precious freedom of the skier in Scotland is allowed because of the acquiescence of landowners. However this desired state of affairs depends upon the skier not interfering with the running of estate activities, or in any way making a nuisance of himself. Should the increase in ski touring activity genuinely cause aggravation to those who depend all year on the land for their living then we can expect landowners to feel the need to protect themselves. We owe it to future generations not to disrupt the current state of affairs.

In particular ski tourers can help by causing the least disruption possible to deer and lambs. Do not disturb deer in winter. If seen in advance, ski away from them. They are weak and vulnerable at this time and causing them to rush away results in unnecessary usage of their vital energy reserves. The deer stalking season for red deer stags is from 1 July to 20 October, and therefore not in the main skiing season. However for red deer hinds the season for culling is from 21 October to 15 February. Between these dates the skier can avoid deer wintering grounds or find out what stalking activities are taking place and not disrupt them. The Mountaineering Council for Scotland and the Scottish Landowners' Federation have compiled a booklet, published by the Scottish Mountaineering Trust entitled *Heading for the Scottish Hills*. This provides a contact list of names and telephone numbers so that information can be sought before embarking on an outing. Lambing generally occurs in April and May.

Ski tourers are generally aware that it is the responsibility of all who go into the countryside to maintain its beauty and not destroy it by their passage. For the most part they obey the Country Code and feel they are innocent of any charges of damage to the landscape. They ski on snow, which melts, and thus they leave no trace of their one-time presence. However, increasing numbers of ski tourers following classic routes is causing damage on the high plateaux. Steel edges cut into vegetation. In spring when snow cover becomes incomplete and skiers hop from snow patch to snow patch they can be crossing vegetation at the most critical time for germination and growth. Compaction of the snow, caused when several skiers follow one track, is also damaging. To reduce such damage skiers can avoid skiing in others' tracks, spread out over the snow on the plateau and limit skiing on vegetation, especially in the spring.

UNDERSTANDING THE FACT SHEETS

A simple fact sheet outlining basic information has been included for each tour.

The times indicated on the fact sheets are intended as a rough guide only. They are calculated at a rate of 4kms per hour plus 1 minute per 10m of ascent. Time for rest stops must be added on to this. Downhill stretches have also been calculated at 4kms per hour. (Some people ski very slowly downhill!) This equation has proven reasonably accurate on many occasions. However, time taken will be affected by many factors. Adjust your own calculations accordingly.

Where information as been categorised the meaning of each category is as outlined below:

Abilities Required - Skiing

No grades of difficulty are given as some tours are easy in terms of techniques required to complete them, yet difficult because of their length or remoteness. In some cases difficulties may be real, but short-lived. Some difficult sections can be walked - thus eliminating the problem. In other cases it may be difficult or dangerous to walk. The individual problems of each tour have been outlined - or the ease with which the tour can be completed.

Abilities Required - Navigational Skills

Elementary Map Reading Skills
> Ability to follow a map
> Plenty of reference points
> Navigational error unlikely to lead into an
> unsafe situation
> Poor visibility rarely a problem

Basic Winter Navigation Skills
> Ability to read a map and use a compass
> Adequate number of reference points
> Poor visibility a possibility

Good Winter Navigation Skills
> Ability to read a map and use a compass
> Limited number of reference points
> Poor visibility not uncommon

Excellent Winter Navigation Skills
> Precise route-finding required
> Cliffs or other dangers near route
> Lack of features as reference points
> Conditions of poor visibility likely

Skiing Equipment Needed

Three categories of skiing gear are recommended to suit the types of terrain the tours cover, light touring, general touring and mountain touring. Using light or general touring gear in mountainous country is very difficult and can be downright dangerous. Using gear from a different category for light or general touring is not as serious, but limits performance and enjoyment.

Light Touring Gear

Skis
Light touring skis are thinner and longer than the other categories of skis. Their length is approximately the skier's height plus 30cms. They have no metal edges and are waisted only slightly. They are ideal for zipping along forest or easy moorland trails, but are hopeless, indeed dangerous, on steep icy mountain sides.

Boots
Light touring boots are lightweight "running shoe look-a-likes". These boots do not provide adequate support for mountain touring.

Bindings
Most sorts of bindings are acceptable, although the current design of three-pin binding is wider than cut tracks. Salomon system or Rottefella New Nordic Norm are bindings on the market suited to this type of touring.

Poles
The approximate length should be the skier's height less 30cms. A half basket is ideal.

General Touring Gear

This gear is suitable for track or moorland terrain, but again not for steep icy mountain sides.

Skis

Medium-weight skis are best for general touring, with the approximate length of the ski measuring the skier's height plus 25cms. They are waisted for turning and may have light (e.g. aluminium) metal edges.

Boots

A medium-weight boot is suitable. Some ankle support is needed, and hence a boot is better than a shoe. A patterned sole is an advantage.

Bindings

Bindings similar to light touring bindings are appropriate although the heavier weight bindings give easier control in descent.

Poles

Most sorts are suitable. The approximate length should be the skier's height less 35cms.

N.B. If conditions are icy steel edges may be preferred, even for tours where light touring or general touring gear is usually suitable.

Mountain Touring Gear

This gear is designed for touring the high peaks and must be able to cope with steep slopes and the worst of snow conditions.

Skis

Mountain touring skis are heavyweight skis, shorter and wider than for the other categories. The approximate ski length should be the skier's height plus 20cms. They should have steel edges to cope with Scottish ice. They are waisted with a softer camber to aid turning. These skis can be used on steep and icy slopes.

Boot

Heavy leather boots, designed to give firm lateral support to the foot in turning, and good ankle support are ideal for mountain touring. The ability to fit crampons is desirable. It is likely you will have to walk to the snow in your boots - make sure they are comfortable and will give you the support you need over the worst terrain. They should have Vibram or other non-slip patterned soles. Gaiters covering the boots and stretching to knee-height are recommended. Safety straps to stop the skis escaping rapidly downhill are essential.

Bindings

Strong touring bindings are necessary. They should be robust and the sidewalls should extend down the boot to increase support.

Poles

The approximate length should be the skier's height less 35cms. The shaft should be made of strong material. Fibreglass is not recommended. Aluminium is ideal. A full circle basket which floats and angles itself to the slope is best. Adjustable straps allow different thicknesses of gloves to be worn. Adjustable poles are becoming popular. They allow a shortening of the pole for steep descents and a longer pole for more push across the plateaux.

A Note on Skins!

Skins are not necessary for mountain touring, but they make ascent of steep slopes so very painless, that they are being increasingly regarded as a standard piece of Nordic mountain touring gear.

Caution

It is extremely important to match skis, boots and bindings. Mixing a heavy ski with a light shoe and binding for example, will cause poor performance and damage to equipment.

I have made no mention of wax or no-wax options. Either are safe in all categories, and the final choice depends upon personal preference.

Other Equipment Needed

It is very much up to the individual what he chooses to carry with him on a ski tour. However, I have indicated one of three categories of equipment for each tour, which I consider it would be sensible to carry - lightweight, light rucksack, and full mountain gear.

Lightweight Equipment

For these tours you may wish to carry nothing more than the route map, given that retreat can be quickly beaten in an emergency or bad weather situation. However, it is always advisable to carry the following when skiing, either in a bum sack or the pockets of a well-designed jacket:

    Chocolate bars or other energy supply
    Spare gloves and hat
    Compass
    Whistle
    Sunglasses
    Sun cream
    Lip salve

Light Rucksack

For tours of several hours duration or short tours into bleak terrain the skier needs to carry enough food and spare clothes to enable him to complete the tour in comfort if the weather deteriorates, or if he sustains an injury or damage to equipment. A small "day sack" containing the following should suffice:

    Relevant maps and compass
    Food and drink for the journey and a small amount for an
     emergency
    Wind and waterproof jacket and overtrousers, spare hat
    and gloves.
    Sun protection
    Torch, whistle, small first aid kit, watch
    Waxes if used.

This is basically a condensed version of the full mountain equipment rucksack.

Full Mountain Equipment

For tours where full mountain equipment is recommended it can be expected that the skier will be away from his base for several hours, possibly encountering dirty weather, taxing terrain and difficult snow conditions. He must carry gear to enable him to safely deal with these eventualities. Full mountain equipment therefore includes:

    Relevant map and compass
    Spare clothing - hats, gloves, spare warm jumper or jacket,
    wind and waterproof jacket and trousers

Food and drink for the journey and an emergency supply
First aid kit
Emergency ski repair kit - spare ski tip, screwdriver, glue, twine, strong sticky tape, possibly spare binding
Sun protection - glasses and cream
Torch and spare battery
Survival bag
Whistle
Watch or clock
Waxes if used

Consider also:

Ice axe and crampons for use on steep and icy slopes
Snow shovel - take if there is any risk of avalanches, also useful for building snow shelter for rest stops or emergencies.
You will probably have to walk to the snow. Means of attaching skis and poles in a neat and safe way onto your rucksack is therefore greatly advantageous.

EXPLANATION OF THE MAPS

The maps are simply an indication of where routes are. They do not replace the maps of the Ordnance Survey, the skier should take the relevant Ordnance Survey Sheet with him on all tours. In particular the sketch maps do not show slope angle or direction, and features away from the route are not included.

Symbols Used

— — — ••••	Route. Short dashes indicate increase in difficulty
• — • — • —	Alternative Route
═══════	Road
───────	Track
〜〜〜	Stream
=	Bridge
⬭	Loch or Lochan
P	Parking
┼┼┼┼─O─┼┼┼┼	Railway Line (and Station)
┝┼┼┼┼┼┤	Ski Tow
⤬─⤬─⤬─	Pylons
→ → → →	Pipeline
△	Summit or High Point
⇞ ⇞ ⇞	Coniferous Forest
♀	Deciduous Woods
▲ ▲ ▲ ▲	Cliff of Crags
■	Building(s)
+	Church
△	Campsite
⌒⌒	Quarry (disused)

THE TOURS, ROUTES AND AREA DESCRIPTIONS

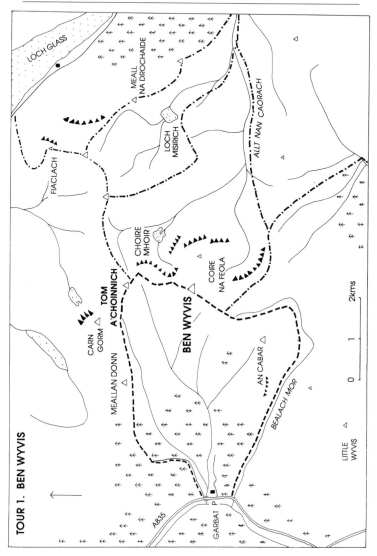

TOUR 1. BEN WYVIS

1. BEN WYVIS

OS SHEET: 20 (21 useful if approaching from the E)

START POINT: Lay-by on W side of A835 at Garbat, GR 412678

TOTAL DISTANCE: 17kms   ASCENT: 990m   TIME: 5 hours 55 minutes

TERRAIN: Forest track and rides leading to mountain slopes of all gradients. Elongated high level grassy ridge, descent down snow bowl to snow-filled burn.

SKIING ABILITIES REQUIRED: Ability to climb, traverse and descend steep slopes and one section of narrow ridge. Ability to ski the distance.

OTHER ABILITIES REQUIRED: Excellent winter navigation and hillcraft skills.

SKIING EQUIPMENT NEEDED: Mountain touring gear.

OTHER EQUIPMENT NEEDED: Full mountain equipment.

SNOW COVER: Good. Grassy base and high altitude of the summit ridge favour a good snow cover. Snow collects in the sheltered, grassy corries, usually allowing skiing well into spring. The geographical location of the mountain means it is influenced by a variety of wind systems each of which has its own pattern of snow distribution. The Moray Firth lies directly to the E and snow-bearing winds from the North Sea are funnelled straight over Ben Wyvis, dropping snow in the sheltered eastern corries and loading the steep W flank of Glas Leathad Mor. However, the warm influence of the sea means the E and NE lose snow quickly. It is a very changeable mountain. It is not unusual to find cornices on both E and W sides of the summit ridge, and it is worth knowing the history of the winds throughout the winter to know where the snow will be. Generally the more grassy E side is thought to be better. Snow cover on the Wyvis landmass can be seen from the A9 S of Inverness. The S and SE facing slopes can be seen from Dingwall, and much of the snow cover on the route described here can be checked from the start point on the A835.

APPROACH ROADS: A835 Dingwall to Ullapool.

Ben Wyvis is generally given a high rating as a ski mountain. Its massive hulk is grassy-based with a broad elongated summit ridge and a number of spur ridges giving good high level skiing. There are fine descents into the snow bowls of wide corries where runs on a variety of slope angles can be found. The potential of the mountain for downhill skiing has been recognised and it has been considered for development with downhill skiing facilities.

Ben Wyvis has the reputation of being avalanche prone, particularly since a ski tourer was fatally injured in an avalanche on the mountain. There is avalanche danger on Ben Wyvis, as there is on other mountains. The grassy base combined with heavy loading of snow on the steep flank of Glas Leathad Mor make this slope suspect. Wind slab is common along the W flank between An Cabar and Carn Gorm, equally so in the burns descending this side, which are otherwise good ski descents. Cornicing is also a danger - the broad summit ridge gives a false sense of security. It can be very narrow to the SW of the main summit. In mist navigation must be precise. Cornices tend to build up at the head of Coire na Feola and Choire Mhoir.

Skiers approach the mountain from the E, S and W. Some of the best routes traverse the mountain, however this requires organisation of transport. From the E access is from Glen Glass (note - this is deer country and hind shooting can continue until mid February. Sensible precautions should be taken). The E section offers an abundance of excellent high level ski routes on broad ridges, such as E of Tom a' Choinnich to Meall nan Bradan Leathan and then N to Fiaclach, or S to Meall na Drochaide; to the E of Choire Mhoir; and above the cliffs S of Coire na Feola. There is usually good running to Loch Misirich well into the spring. Extensive new planting has occurred on the slopes W of Glen Glass and Loch Glass between the road end at Eileanach Lodge and Culzie Lodge making routes to the skiing grounds from this side difficult. Until these are established through the forest, detours to the N and along the Loch Glass track or S to the Allt nan Caorach tracks and to the Glen Glass road at Redburn are lengthy alternatives.

The approaches from the S are long, but snow holds surprisingly well in some of the S-flowing burns. It is possible to see the snowline from Dingwall or the main A835 and A834 roads. The minor road running N of the A834 between Dingwall and Strathpeffer is the usual start point, from where routes ascend gradually through forest and across moor to steeper slopes, the eastern corries, and the broad summit ridges.

The approach from the W is very popular. The usual start point is Garbat on the A835. From here much of the W flank of the main ridge can be seen and a route chosen according to snow cover and stability, and slope angle. The slopes immediately N and W of An Cabar are steep and usually blown clear. An Cabar is a popular approach for hillwalkers, but is not a good ski option. The slopes between here and Tom a'Choinnich are steep and dressed frequently with suspect wind slab. There are more gentle approaches, better suited to Nordic Skis at the N end, towards Carn Gorm. A worthwhile circuit links these and a summit ascent with one of the best descents on the mountain down the course of the Allt a' Bhealaich Mhoir. For snow cover and terrain it is one of the most suitable routes on the mountain for Nordic skiers.

The start point is the lay-by on the A835 at Garbat. Immediately to the N is Garbat Bridge, and to the N of this a forest track leads NE into Garbat Forest. This ascends steadily through the trees. From where it terminates fire breaks can be followed NE to the forest edge. There has been new planting in the former clearing W of Meallan Donn. In descent the ride leading back to the forest road is not immediately obvious and will become decreasingly so as the trees grow.

From the forest edge easy slopes lead E to Meallan Donn. Ascend the easiest line to the ridge between Carn Gorm and Tom a' Choinnich and then more steeply SE to the summit of Tom a' Choinnich.

The route continues from Tom a' Choinnich to the main summit of Ben Wyvis. This is straightforward, exhilarating high level skiing in clear conditions, offering extensive, spectacular views. In mist it requires careful, precise navigation.

From the summit the route follows the ridge SW. Immediately after the summit this ridge narrows, with steep drops on either side. It calls for competent skiing and navigational skills.

Continue SW, until well past Coire na Feola a broad snow bowl opens out to the S. This coire contains the upper waters of the Allt a' Bhealaich Mhoir, which flows S and then curves around W to the Bealach Mor. To follow the course of these waters gives an excellent descent. When the snow expires the Bealach Mor track leads back to Garbat Forest. A path leads alongside Allt a' Bhealaich Mhoir to the A835 0.5km S of the start point. Fire breaks and forest roads can be used to descend the forest to the A835 at Garbat. However these tend to be wet, boggy and less attractive than the good path alongside the Allt a' Bhealaich Mhoir.

CLASHINDARROCH FOREST

Clashindarroch Forest offers some of the best forest skiing in Scotland. It is situated in Strathbogie engulfing a vast area of upland W of Rhynie and Huntly. There are many kilometres of track threading deep into the forest, and a variety of short, and interesting circuits close to the road. The 1:50,000 scale OS maps of this area do not show sufficient detail of these to assist route planning or navigation whilst in the forest, but the tracks and rides are shown on the 1:25,000 scale OS maps and much fun can be had exploring the forest maze with their help.

The best access is from the A941 Rhynie to Dufftown road, which skirts the S part of the forest, and which rises to over 400m. It is kept open in all but the worst of conditions. Since it rises above the average height of the forest it is not necessary to go away from the road to seek better snow.

There are several entrances into the forest along the stretch of road running E from the junction with the B9002, although as the popularity of the area grows parking may become difficult at some of these.

The forest tracks have quite remarkable snow-holding properties, possibly the best in the United Kingdom. Snow cover can be extremely good even after a period of thaw elsewhere. Indeed, it is quite often the case that the surrounding area is devoid of snow and the approaches bone dry. However, only a short distance into the forest there is a network of skiable tracks. The height of the forest above sea level and the shade provided by the tall trees are partly responsible for preserving the snow, however the accumulations of snow on the tracks requires further explanation. One theory for this is that falling snow is blown across the tops of the trees, but upon reaching a ride or track turbulence causes it to fall. In general the season stretches from late December to March, although it is sometimes possible to ski as early as November. The well graded tracks and grassy nature of

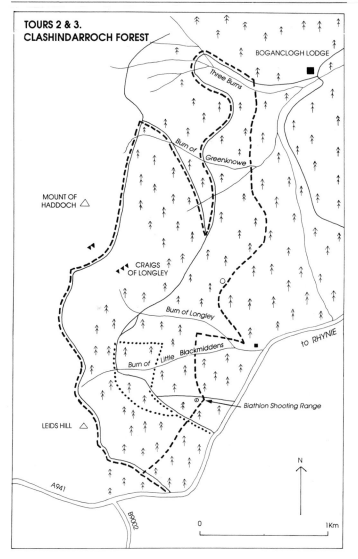

TOURS 2 & 3.
CLASHINDARROCH FOREST

BOGANCLOGH LODGE

Three Burns

Burn of Greenknowe

MOUNT OF HADDOCH △

CRAIGS OF LONGLEY

Burn of Longley

to RHYNIE

Burn of Little Blackmiddens

Biathlon Shooting Range

LEIDS HILL △

A941

B9002

N

0   1Km

the rides mean skiing is possible with only thin snow cover.

The excellent skiing potential has made the area very popular and it is usual to have other people's tracks to follow. A number of races are held here and the forest is currently the chosen venue for races organised by the Armed Forces. There is a biathlon shooting range at GR 426268.

This is commercial forest plantation, and although there is a mix of conifers represented, they are generally planted in uninspiring rows of identical trees of uniform height. For the most part they obliterate any view of the surrounding uplands.

The forest has been extended further W than shown on the OS maps available at the time of writing. The E flanks of Leids Hill and Mount of Haddoch have been planted giving forest cover up to 500m and therefore some excellent future skiing potential. Until the trees here grow this will be an area offering views of the surrounding uplands, in particular of The Buck to the S and Tap O' Noth to the E.

There are two significant tracks that are not shown on the current OS maps in the main skiing area N of the A941. One leads from the road into the forest from GR 427266 to join with one of the main routes running N. The second forks from this at GR 426280 and curves NW to join the upper track below Mount of Haddoch just N of the Burn of Greenknowe. It should also be noted that not all the ridges shown on the maps are suitable and that the workings of the Forestry Commission can render areas unskiable.

There is access to the forest from the N and E from a series of minor public roads. They do not rise as high as the A941 and generally the snow cover in these parts is much inferior to that of the main skiing area. However, given a recent fall of snow at 200m there is a vast amount of exploring to be done from these road ends. The 1:25,000 OS Sheet NJ 43/53 Huntly (South) covers this area.

There is also skiing in the forest at Gartly Moor (also shown on Sheet NJ 43/53) where there are official ski trails waymarked. In general, opinion regards this area to be inferior to the main Clashindarroch Forest.

There is a small area of forest S of the A941 in Grid Square 4427. It holds snow reasonably well and is popular with beginners as the tracks are easy and ideal for learning on.

For a more adventurous outing The Buck lies S of the forest and holds snow in ribbons above the Burn of Buck. A pleasant ascent route from the B9002 follows the valley of Burn of Buck to the col between the summit and Kebbuck Knowe from where easy skiing leads to the summit. There is a fine run down the outward route.

There are so many skiing options within the forest that the skier should have no difficulty finding his own route of exploration, aided by the OS map. Indeed such exploration is the main joy of touring in Clashindarroch Forest. However, two particularly good routes are suggested here, covering the best snowholding area, one a fairly long route, the other short, but of great character.

2. ROUTE 1 - CLASHINDARROCH FOREST

OS SHEET: 1:25,000 NJ 42/52, Rhynie

START POINT: Entrance to Forest, GR 424261

TOTAL DISTANCE: 11kms   ASCENT: 240m   TIME: 3 hours

TERRAIN: Forest road, tracks and rides. Some ascent and descent.

SKIING ABILITIES REQUIRED: Mostly very easy terrain, but some basic uphill and downhill technique required.

OTHER ABILITIES REQUIRED: Elementary map reading skills.

SKIING EQUIPMENT NEEDED: Light touring gear.

OTHER EQUIPMENT NEEDED: Lightweight equipment.

SNOW COVER: Good. Season December to March. Upper track holds snow less well than in the established forest - but this will improve as the trees here grow. Even on this upper track the cover is good when drifting from the moor creates a skiable ribbon along its length.

APPROACH ROADS: A941 Rhynie to Dufftown road. Limited roadside parking.

Follow the Land-Rover track NW into the forest and ascend towards Leids Hill. Continue along this broad track past Craigs of Longley and below Mount of Haddoch until a downhill stretch leads to a junction with a forest road just beyond the Burn of Greenknowe. At the time of writing this upper track leads through an area recently planted. It is therefore different in character to routes within the previously established forest. It holds the snow fairly well and there

Forest road skiing, Clashindarroch Forest (Tour 2)

are some downhill runs to compensate for uphill pulls. It offers views across the forest sprawl and surrounding uplands.

Turn right at the junction and descend gradually the forest road for 1km SSW to a junction with the main route running N/S. Turn sharply left (N) and follow the track for 1.5kms until it bends round in a broad 'U' turn to the right at Three Burns. This forest road continues to Boganclogh Lodge, however the route bears S 0.5km before the lodge along a broad ride. This leads off to the right at GR 431293 and has a weight limit notice at its entrance. It gives very good running on a grassy base between tall trees, which provide excellent shade for the snow, and is followed for 2kms to the Burn of Longley. Note that just S of the stone circle, GR 428277, there is a fork and ride not shown on the OS map. By continuing straight on at the fork, and bearing left at the next junction, maintaining a generally S direction, the T-junction by the Burn of Longley GR 430272 is reached after 0.5km. From here a left turn leads promptly to the A941, however the route bears right to cross the burn and ascend W for 300m distance to the first ride leading S. This is followed, the Burn of Little Blackmiddens crossed, and a T-junction with the forest road reached. The biathlon range is immediately to the W along this road. Again a left turn leads to the A941 but the route goes straight across and ascends steeply SW. It continues to run parallel to the A941, crossing other roads and rides leading back to the main road, until the outward route is met just N of the start point and the final short descent on the forest road made.

3. ROUTE 2 - CLASHINDARROCH FOREST

OS SHEET: 1:25,000 NJ 42/52, Rhynie

START POINT: Entrance to forest, GR 427266

TOTAL DISTANCE: 2.5kms   ASCENT: 70m   TIME: 45 minutes

TERRAIN: Forest roads and rides. Undulating gradient. One short steep section.

SKIING ABILITIES REQUIRED: Vast repertoire of skills useful, but even those with little ability can have fun attempting this one.

OTHER ABILITIES REQUIRED: Elementary map reading skills.

SKIING EQUIPMENT NEEDED: Light touring gear.

OTHER EQUIPMENT NEEDED: Lightweight equipment.

SNOW COVER: Good. Season December to March.

APPROACH ROADS: A941 Rhynie to Dufftown road.

This is a short route serving as an introduction to the trails close to the A941 road. It has much character and a high enjoyment score.

From the entrance to the forest by the boom across the forest road (not marked on OS maps at the time of writing) ski easily W. At the point where the forest road begins to descend, a ride forks to the left and arcs NW for 1km. This has earned the name "The Rollercoaster", as it undulates its course through the forest. The larches alongside spread their branches across the ride. If not pruned they render passage difficult.

The ride rejoins the forest road, which is then followed N for 200m distance to a junction where another ride crosses the forest road. Turn right and ski E. This is a pleasant downhill run. Turn right at the T-junction and cross the Burn of Little Blackmiddens to return once again to the forest road. Turn left and follow the forest road steeply again to return to the start point.

4. THE LECHT

OS SHEETS: 36 and 37

The A939 Lecht Road rises to a height of 635m above sea level, and so offers skiers good access to a snow-bearing area. The road blocks easily and the "Cock Bridge to Tomintoul" section is repeatedly reported closed in winter. However the authorities do attempt to keep the route open. The access to snowy slopes has attracted some downhill skiing development with machinery and snow fencing at the top of the Pass. At the moment it is limited in size. The runs are short and not too difficult - suitable for Nordic downhill practice.

1. The Ladder Hills

Stretching NE from the Lecht is a ridge of elongated summits, the Ladder Hills. This ridge is quickly reached by a short stiff climb up the steep slopes E of the Pass, from here a lengthy traverse undulates gently above the 700m contour line. To traverse the Ladder Hills is an easy ski tour at an elevated height offering extensive views to the Cairngorms, the Hills of Cromdale and Ben Rinnes and the Whisky Glens. Mostly the running over the summits is good, with a short grass and mossy base, but peat hags at low points may be a problem if they are not filled with snow.

The ridge may be blown clear in which case snow ribbons on the lee side (usually the E flanks) are an alternative. A fence leads from the road up to the ridge at Meikle Corr Riabhach and extends along the route to Carn Liath. N of this summit it descends NW from a cairn down the mountain's broad NW ridge. To this point it provides a very useful indicator of the route in poor visibility. The tour continues NE however to the OS column on Carn Mor, the highest point of the Ladder Hills. From this summit there is a view to the Braes of Glenlivet and the distillery at Chapeltown. It is possible to continue to the peat hags of Dun Muir, beyond which the running improves

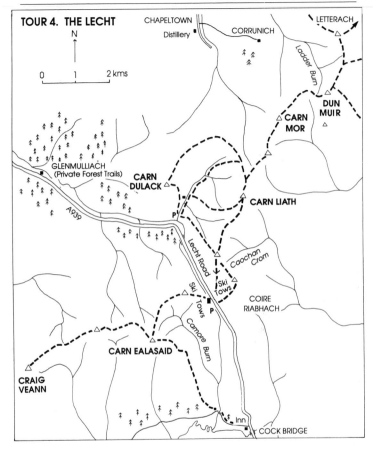

TOUR 4. THE LECHT

N

0   1   2 kms

CHAPELTOWN

Distillery

CORRUNICH

LETTERACH

Ladder Burn

CARN MOR

DUN MUIR

GLENMULLIACH
(Private Forest Trails)

CARN DULACK

CARN LIATH

A939

Lecht Road

Caochan Crom

Ski Tows

P

COIRE RIABHACH

Ski Tows

P

Carnore Burn

CARN EALASAID

CRAIG VEANN

Inn

COCK BRIDGE

again and routes can be taken N over broad and easy slopes to Letterach or NE to Geal Charn. To return to the start point the best running follows the outward tracks to just N of Meikle Corr Riabhach then traverses the slopes above the A939 on a descending line S to the snow fencing and machinery of the downhill pistes. Alternatively downhill running can be enjoyed over the moorland wastes E of the route, climbing back on gentle slopes to Meikle Corr Riabhach up the valley of the Caochan Crom. The burns hereabouts may be engulfed in steep snow banks, and holding cornices. The Allt an t-Sluichd Mhoir and the Allt Slochd Chaimbeil have incised deeply, but the moors between them offer wide spacious slopes.

It is possible to descend W to the Braes of Glenlivet and the road at Chapeltown, where the distillery offers an interesting destination. A hill track descends the Ladder Burn from N of Dun Muir to Corrunich, but this is only mentioned as a useful escape route. The slopes are steep here, and the valley is narrow and restricting. There is better running from Carn na Glascoill, N of Letterach to the Burn of Coirebreac and Ladderfoot. This does require good snow cover on the deep heathery slopes, and snow may well run out well before Ladderfoot is reached.

The minor road leading N to Glenbuchat Lodge from the B973 Strathdon Road rises to 410m above sea level. It is a good launch pad to broad and gentle snow slopes leading from the highest point at GR 335174 W to Moss Hill and then NW to the main line of hills between Dun Muir and Geal Charn. Alternatively from this road a path to Dun Muir leads N of the Water of Nochty to Aldachuie and the ruin of Duffdefiance. This route may give good skiing, particularly as the forest assists snow holding.

2. To the W of the A939

There is often good skiing on the hills W of the Lecht Road. From Beinn a' Chruinnich a route leads via Carn Ealasaid and Tolm Buirich to Craig Veann. The terrain is easy Nordic country of gentle, spacious slopes, broad flat-topped ridges and rounded summits. The hills are slightly lower than those NE of the Lecht, but otherwise very similar in character. Moss and short heather give good rock-free running, but peaty depressions and some long heather disrupts this in places. Summits are often blown clear. The moors are desolate, uninspiring places in mist, but otherwise give rewarding views of the Eastern Cairngorms. The Camore Burn, which drains the slopes between Beinn a' Chruinnich and Carn Ealasaid traps the snow and there is usually skiing on the slopes around its headwaters until April. The slopes to the W of the burn on the E side of Carn Ealasaid hold snow, and wraiths often extend along the E flanks of the S shoulder. Thus a ski descent can often be made from the summit of Carn Ealasaid, holding above the Camore Burn, to join hill tracks descending to Loinherry and then to the Inn at Cock Bridge. This shoulder can be seen from the A939 E of Cock Bridge and the snow cover checked. If snow cover here is poor this is difficult walking terrain of long heather on steep slopes, although the hill tracks, if reached assist greatly.

3. Coire Riabhach

This coire lies E of the A939, just S of the downhill skiing area. It holds snow well, and gives sheltered, peaceful skiing on a variety of slope gradients, often until April.

4. Well of the Lecht

N of the Pass where the road bends sharply W there is a car park and picnic area, GR 234152. At 460m above sea level it is 175m lower than the highest point on the pass. However if snow is lying here it makes an attractive focal point for a ski tour. A track leads upstream to the well-preserved building of a former iron works, an interesting edifice. Beyond this the burn can be followed N and the head of the valley ascended. The slopes are wide and easy, but long heather gives a difficult base in early season or lean conditions. The fence posts are gained giving an obvious route to Carn Liath. A circular route around the valley offers a short excursion, with pleasant and easy skiing along the tops. This ascends the broad ridge leading E from the iron works to Carn Liath, from where the fence posts are followed N around the head of the valley. It sweeps SW towards Carn Dulack to descend steepening slopes back to the car park.

5. Glenmullie

At the time of writing a Nordic Centre operates at Glenmulliach, SE of Tomintoul, offering 25kms of waymarked trails. Tracks are cut.

Skiing on the sheltered forest roads

These are private and skiers are charged a fee for the use of facilities and trails. A map of routes is available from the Centre.

5. ABERNETHY FOREST

OS SHEET: 36

START POINT: End of public road just after Dell Lodge, GR 011193

TOTAL DISTANCE: 13kms   ASCENT: 170m   TIME: 3 hours 30 minutes

TERRAIN: Broad, well-graded forest roads, predominantly easy gradients.

SKIING ABILITIES REQUIRED: Majority of the tour is very easy and suitable for beginners.

OTHER ABILITIES REQUIRED: Elementary map reading skills.

SKIING EQUIPMENT NEEDED: Light touring gear.

OTHER EQUIPMENT NEEDED: Lightweight equipment.

SNOW COVER: Dependent on snow lying at low levels - tour lies between 240m and 400m above sea level. Short season, usually confined to the winter months.

APPROACH ROADS: B970 to Nethy Bridge. Minor road immediately S of the bridge over the River Nethy to Dell Lodge.

This is an easy tour, suitable for beginners and children. It penetrates into the Abernethy Forest, the largest area of Caledonian Forest remaining in Scotland. Natural regeneration of plant life is encouraged here, and it is pleasant to ski between open stances of spreading Scots pines. There are some fine views, but in particular at Rynettin, from where there is an interesting view of the Cairngorms. The tour can quite easily be shortened, lengthened or reversed.

The route combines two loops in a figure of eight, with Forest Lodge at the centre. The second loop, S of the Lodge, contains ascent and descent, although the difficulties are not serious, and as this section rises to 400m it is more promising for snow cover. However, the absolute beginner or confidence building skier may wish to complete the easy first loop only (8kms, 2 hours).

Each loop can be skied in either direction. For the first the anti-clockwise direction gives one short section of fast downhill running. There is a run out, but the less able may prefer walking this, to

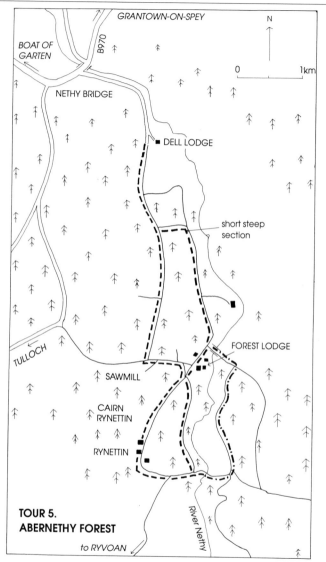

TOUR 5.
ABERNETHY FOREST

uncontrolled excitement. If skied in a clockwise direction everyone should be able to keep skis on all the way round (snow permitting). For the second loop the anticlockwise choice gives a pleasant descent after Rynettin, whereas the clockwise route means descending the restricting track and forest back to the Lodge. The following notes describe the full route when skied anticlockwise.

From the end of the public road just after Dell Lodge enter the forest on the broad track and ski S for 3kms through pleasant stances of Scots pines to a T-junction. Turn left onto another broad forest road which leads to Forest Lodge. Just before the Lodge there is a junction of tracks by a sign and information board depicting the National Nature Reserve. The board shows trails within the Reserve, which can also be explored on skis. This point is the centre of the figure of eight. The second loop begins here and returns to this point.

To include the second loop turn right through the deer fence gate and then bear right again, keeping the fence on your right and some power lines to your left. The track climbs steadily and although still broad, it is not as well-graded as that so far travelled. Views over the Nethy Valley and Forest to the Hills of Cromdale can be snatched through the pines. If descending this route requires control as the path makes an S bend on a steep section.

The forest opens on the left to reveal Carn Bheadhair to the E and then gradually the Cairngorm Massif to the S. The three buildings at Rynettin mark the highest point on the tour. One is open and offers sound shelter from the weather. Unfortunately the animals hereabouts also appreciate this and salubriousness is lacking. It is worth visiting Rynettin for the view.

Descend E from Rynettin to join the broad track from Ryvoan. This descent is over open grassy terrain and not steep. Follow the track E to a junction of tracks above the River Nethy. It is possible to ski back to Forest Lodge along the good track on the far bank of the Nethy. This however involves an adventurous river crossing. For less drama turn left at the junction and follow the easy track N through the pines to return to Forest Lodge.

Pass by the buildings of Forest Lodge to gain the junction of paths by the bridge over the Nethy. From here turn N along the easy broad track to where it bends W and descends to join the outward route 1km from the start point. This short section of descent after the bend is steep, the track is a bed of rubble, and there is little room for error at the sides. There is a run out, so it can be quite fun in good snow and with adequate skills. If these are not present, you will probably be better off walking this section. Regain the outward route and retrace your tracks to the start point.

6. AROUND THE KINCARDINE HILLS

OS SHEET: 36   START POINT: B970 N of Pityoulish, GR 933152
TOTAL DISTANCE: 28kms   ASCENT: 300m   TIME: 7 hours 30 minutes

TERRAIN: Broad tracks through forest and open terrain. Undulating. Minor back roads. 1.5kms along B970.

SKIING ABILITIES REQUIRED: Ability to cope with the distance. Moderate skills of ascent and descent. Ability to cope if track is icy.

OTHER ABILITIES REQUIRED: Elementary map reading skills.

SKIING EQUIPMENT NEEDED: Light touring gear - unless icy.

OTHER EQUIPMENT NEEDED: Light rucksack.

SNOW COVER: Unreliable. Route is low lying. Requires a good snow fall in the glens to be completely skiable. Tracks frequently icy due to exposure to the sun.

APPROACH ROADS: B970 Coylumbridge to Nethy Bridge. Roadside parking only.

This is a classic low level traverse, circumnavigating the Kincardine Hills. Both the distance and the terrain challenge the track skier. It is an accessible route, along excellent tracks and through varied scenery. Here one can escape the enclosed atmosphere of the more popular Glen More trails.

About one-quarter of the route is along roads. However these are for the most part back roads, which do not receive priority for snow clearance. The authorities clear main roads and bus routes first, only then turning attention to such back roads. Farmers may clear these roads, and the passage of traffic destroys the quality of the skiing, but invariably it is possible to ski here. The short section along the B970 is awkward - and not usually skiable - but necessary in the absence of connecting transport. The best time to ski the road section is early,

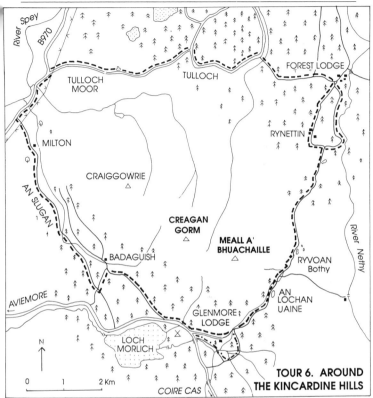

TOUR 6. AROUND THE KINCARDINE HILLS

thus the given choice of start point. This allows all the roads to be skied first. However it is also popular to start in Glen More and ski the route anticlockwise. It may be argued that the clockwise direction affords better views, particularly of the Cairngorms when crossing from Rynettin to Ryvoan.

From the lane end leading to Milton Farm walk 1.5kms N along the B970, to the unobtrusive junction with the minor road heading E. This climbs to cross the weather-beaten Tulloch Moor. To the N the RSPB protects the area. To the S the Kincardines stretch away and indicate the extent of the tour. Juniper bushes, birches and heather abound

47

and there is an atmosphere of wildlife and freedom.

Continue to a road junction and turn S to Tulloch, a small hamlet. The road turns E here and then undulates through farmed land to the woods of Abernethy Forest. Enter the Forest at GR 998166. This completes the road skiing.

An excellent, easy track leads E to Forest Lodge. Abernethy Forest is one of Scotland's finest forests, the largest of the old Caledonian pine forests. Protected by the RSPB, it provides a natural habitat for birds and wild animals. It is a lovely place to ski.

Just before Forest Lodge, pass through the deer fence and follow Route 5 to Rynettin. This involves some ascent, but there are good views from Rynettin, and a pleasant 40m of descent immediately thereafter. For an easier alternative along superior track and with views over the River Nethy go E of the power lines and follow the broad track S to rejoin the route below Rynettin. From here the route follows the old Thieves' Path from Glen More to Nethy Bridge via Ryvoan. The track is good and undulates over fluvo-glacial terrain and through natural forest. Ahead is a fine vista of the Cairngorm Mountains beyond picturesque kettle-hole topography. Glacial and post-glacial features reveal vividly the frozen history of this wild place and the impact ice has had by scooping out earth and spreading it randomly about. Ryvoan Bothy is a welcome half-way point.

The section between the bothy and the junction with the track to Bynack Stable is steep and stony. It faces the sun and is prone to icing. However this section is short, and the track reverts to its excellent broad, but undulating character. Enter the classic glaciated form of Ryvoan Pass. An Lochan Uaine is cupped graciously on the flat valley floor - but may appear quite a different colour to its summer green shade - from which it is named. Follow the "Green Loch" trail to Glenmore Lodge. This is a deservedly popular trail and may well be busy or cluttered with other skiers' tracks. From Glenmore Lodge continue W to join the "Ski Road" at Glen More. The road to Glenmore Lodge may have been cleared, and so for those wishing to maintain the pleasures of good tracks, a longer route can be taken via Route 9 (1km extra). Turn S before the Thieves' Path crosses the Allt na Feith Duibhe. After 1.5kms turn NE and reach the "Ski Road" where it crosses the Abhainn Riugh-eunachan.

A short ski NW through the hubbub at Glen More leads to the start of the Badaguish trails and the route back via An Slugan. Ski NW from the tea shop by the campsite to Badaguish, but turn SW immediately before the cluster of buildings, to follow another easy track to link with the Sluggan Trail. Follow this N through the commercially-planted Queen Elizabeth Forest and onto the deep and steep sides of the Slugan Pass. The Milton Burn trickles insignificantly below. It is a misfit stream not responsible for this deep gash. The Pass was formed by a glacial breakthrough as pressure in Glen More grew. It is quite different in character to the Ryvoan Pass.

Once through the Pass the circumnavigation of the Kincardine Hills is completed. A pretty descent, steep in places, leads down through pines, birches and juniper bushes to fields and the start point.

GLEN MORE FOREST PARK

Glen More Forest Park has become one of the main centres for Nordic activity in the United Kingdom. Proximity to the ski resort of Aviemore, the Nordic Ski School and Inverdruie, and Glenmore Lodge National Outdoor Training Centre have contributed to the popularity. Certainly there is much to favour the forest for skiing. It lies above 300m above sea level in a snow-bearing area. The tall trees preserve the snow, and there is usually skiing for a core season of five to six weeks (January and February) with opportunist skiing between November and April. There are broad easy tracks which can be joined to give circular ski tours whilst links with the forests of Rothiemurchus, Inshriach and Abernethy allow long tours. One very long tour from Feshiebridge follows forest and moorland tracks through Inshriach, Rothiemurchus, Glen More and Abernethy forests to Nethy Bridge.

Waymarkers indicate where some of the routes go, and how difficult they are. In places tracks are cut - indeed Glen More was one of the first places in Britain to have cut-tracks. The forest S of Loch Morlich is the current choice of venue for the United Kingdom Cross-Country Skiing Championships, held in February.

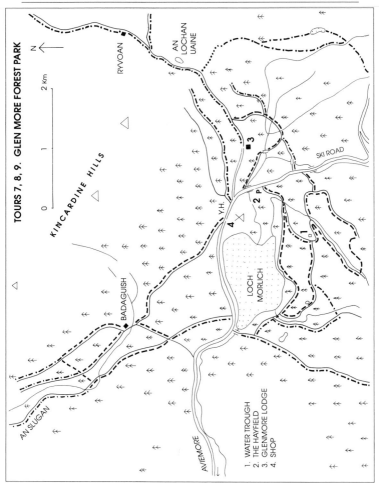

TOURS 7, 8, 9. GLEN MORE FOREST PARK

KINCARDINE HILLS

N

0   1   2 Km

RYVOAN

AN LOCHAN UAINE

SKI ROAD

Y.H.

BADAGUISH

AN SLUGAN

AVIEMORE

LOCH MORLICH

1. WATER TROUGH
2. THE HAYFIELD
3. GLENMORE LODGE
4. SHOP

51

7. THE QUEEN'S FOREST -
TRAILS AROUND BADAGUISH, GLEN MORE

OS SHEET: 36   START POINT: Shop and Tea Room, GR 974098

TOTAL DISTANCE: 9kms (can be shortened or lengthened)

ASCENT: 130m   TIME: 2 hours 30 minutes

TERRAIN: Forest roads. One section of rough terrain on broad forest ride.

SKIING ABILITIES REQUIRED: Most of tour very easy - suitable for beginners. More challenging sections, requiring control on slopes in a restricted area can be walked or by-passed.

OTHER ABILITIES REQUIRED: Elementary map reading skills.

SKIING EQUIPMENT NEEDED: Light touring gear.

OTHER EQUIPMENT NEEDED: Lightweight equipment.

SNOW COVER: Short season, usually confined to the winter months. Trees help to preserve the snow. Tracks skiable with minimum cover - but not the rides.

APPROACH ROADS: Aviemore to Coire Cas "Ski Road".

N of Loch Morlich the Queen's Forest extends along the lower slopes of the Kincardine Hills towards the steep-sided Slugan Pass. Forest roads penetrate towards a cluster of buildings at Badaguish, beyond which three roads lead NW roughly parallel to each other. The most westerly is a through route to the B970 and Pityoulish, used by Tour 6, the other two terminate at the forest fence. The tracks are broad and well-graded and can be linked to give several kilometres of skiing. There are three established ski trails here, with waymarkers indicating direction and difficulty - the "Badaguish Trail" (yellow, easy); the "Sluggan Trail" (also yellow, easy); and the "Canadian Trail" (red, difficult). They combine to give this tour, which can be skied in any direction, with the possibility of omitting difficult sections as necessary. If included these more tricky sections provide stimulating and entertaining skiing.

From the tea shop cross the "Ski Road" and enter the forest along a broad forest road, rising at first, but soon levelling out to give 2kms of easy skiing through thick forest plantation to Badaguish. Just before entering the clearing and buildings turn left onto another broad forest road, which leads to a crossroads. A left turn here leads back to join the Ski Road 1.5kms W of the start point, by a picnic place on the shore of Loch Morlich. It gives easy skiing, ideal for beginners. To continue straight ahead also leads back to the Ski Road 1km even further towards Aviemore. This track has a rubble base and requires a good covering of snow to be skiable.

The main route goes right (N) along the easy Sluggan Trail. It is possible to continue through the Slugan Pass to the Spey Valley. It is a pretty route, particularly in the latter part after leaving the Queen's Forest, where it descends through pine woods, juniper scrub, birches and pasture towards the River Spey. However, after 1.5kms the main route follows a ride leading up to the right, just after the track crosses the Milton Burn and before it passes through a fence. The ride is waymarked. It is a short uphill pull to connect with the middle of the three tracks. This can be crossed and the ride and waymarkers followed further uphill to the upper track and the Canadian Trail. Unlike the main forest roads which are skiable with minimum snow cover, these connecting rides require a good cover to be easily skiable. The upper ride in particular supports a healthy under-growth, but both have tree stumps along their course which can be problematic if the rides are descended at speed. The rides are broad and clear of forest debris, and give testing but interesting skiing in descent.

Either the middle or upper tracks can be followed back to Badaguish. The middle track is suitable for beginners and undulates pleasantly to a junction with the upper Canadian Trail just N of the buildings. The upper track has a marginal advantage of height, so may have more snow. It is a pleasant run back with views to the Cairngorms for those able to cope with a long descent interrupted by short steep sections of possibly icy track.

Both these tracks can be followed easily to the forest boundary to the N. The middle one is overgrown in sections beyond the connecting rides, but is passable and gives occasional views across An Slugan. From the termination point there are interesting views across the Spey to the Monadhliath - the upper track offering a more extensive view.

Return through the building and activity area of Badaguish and follow the outward route back to the start point.

8. SERPENTS LOCH TRAIL - GLEN MORE

OS SHEET: 36

START POINT: Heron's Field Car Park (also known as "The Hayfield" Car Park) GR 980092

TOTAL DISTANCE: 9kms - can be lengthened or shortened

ASCENT: 110m   TIME: 2 hours 30 minutes

TERRAIN: Forest roads. Short section across open terrain, but tracks may have been cut here. Some ascent and descent - short steep sections.

SKIING ABILITIES REQUIRED: Basic ascent and descent skills - but possible with limited skills as more challenging sections can be walked.

OTHER ABILITIES REQUIRED: Elementary map reading skills.

SKIING EQUIPMENT NEEDED: Light touring gear.

OTHER EQUIPMENT NEEDED: Lightweight equipment.

SNOW COVER: Short season - best chances in January and February. Trees shade the snow. Tracks skiable with minimum cover. One of the best bets at this height in the neighbourhood.

APPROACH ROADS: Aviemore to Coire Cas "Ski Road".

This tour is more correctly a combination of the official "Serpents Loch Trail" and the "Allt Rabhaig Trail" starting at the Wayfaring, Heron's Field car park. It is very popular and there may well be tracks cut along the full route. Some of the route has been chosen as the course for the United Kingdom Cross-Country Skiing Championships. That does not mean it is difficult - but there are some sections of moderate ascent and descent. Popularity is more due to the fact that attention has been attracted by waymarking and the races, than to scenic appeal. Views of Loch Morlich are sadly short-lived and practically the whole trail is encased in a forest grown for commercial exploitation. The trails on the other side of the "Ski Road" are more interesting.

The area immediately N of the car park is known as The Hayfield and when snow-covered is an excellent nursery area. There is a level area for flat work and a slope for ascent and descent practice. If the "Ski Road" to Coire Cas is closed this area becomes very busy with "downhill" classes.

There are alternative start points. The route can be approached from the W end of Loch Morlich via the track to Rothiemurchus Lodge, bearing SE after 300m to join the route by the boundary of the Rothiemurchus and Glen More Forests. This is a more pleasant way into the forest, with views to the downhill ski corries, and across Loch Morlich to the Kincardine Hills. There are also interesting links from the campsite at the E end of Loch Morlich. Sinuous but easy routes meander along the shoreline and through the trees to join the main route by the SE corner of Loch Morlich.

From the Wayfaring car park follow the forest track W to a junction 0.5kms from the start point. Take the right fork leading down to Loch Morlich and the links with the campsite. Ski easily for over 1km to a bend in the track at a junction. This is where the Rothiemurchus alternative joins the main route. Go left and ascend past the Serpents Loch, climbing to a junction by a concrete trough. It is also possible to go straight on at the bend, crossing into Rothiemurchus Forest, and then turning left up another good, but less popular track to a side track. This leads NE to rejoin the main route just E of the Serpents Loch. It is a quieter alternative but of little other value, especially as the track disappears briefly by the deer fence boundary, where it crosses back into Glen More Forest. (Route finding on this section easier going W to E.)

From the water trough a left turn (N) leads back to the start point, but includes a steep, restricted section requiring control or a sense of humour. The main route turns right to follow easily the broad track up the Allt Rabhaig. This extends to the forest boundary from where explorative off-track skiing of a more demanding nature can be enjoyed through open woods and beyond on heather moors, perhaps including a visit to Lochan Dubh a' Chadha. However, the main route crosses the Allt Rabhaig just before the forest boundary, to escape the morbid forest and traverse more open terrain E until waymarkers lead back to the forest and another track. This leads gently down NE to a main junction. Turning right the track descends, steeply in parts to the "Ski Road" which can be followed back to the start point. For a longer route back, avoiding the roadside skiing, turn left and return to the water trough and follow the difficult run back to the outward route and the car park.

9. GREEN LOCH AND OTHER TRAILS EAST OF SKI ROAD - GLEN MORE

OS SHEET: 36

START POINT: Heron's Field Car Park ("The Hayfield") GR 980092

TOTAL DISTANCE: 7.5kms   ASCENT: 40m   TIME: 2 hours

TERRAIN: Forest roads, easy gradients.

SKIING ABILITIES REQUIRED: Suitable for beginners.

OTHER ABILITIES REQUIRED: Elementary map reading skills.

SKIING EQUIPMENT NEEDED: Light touring gear.

OTHER EQUIPMENT NEEDED: Lightweight equipment.

SNOW COVER: Short season, dependent on snow at 350m. Trees help to preserve the snow, but some forest has been cleared recently, and parts of the route go through more open forest. Thus snow holding is not as good as elsewhere in Glen More Forest Park. Tracks skiable with minimum cover.

APPROACH ROADS: Aviemore to Coire Cas Ski Road.

The trails E of the "Ski Road" do not join to give circular ski tours as do trails elsewhere in the forest. They are more open, which means the snow is not as well preserved by shading, and that the skier is not as well protected from the weather. However, they are the prettiest of the Glen More trails, they are easy, and they have not as yet been spoiled by racing circuits and track-cutting machinery. There are sections leading through the Caledonian Pine Reserve, trails beside burns radiating from the Northern Corries of Cairn Gorm, quaint footbridges, fluvo-glacial scenery, and of course, Ryvoan Pass itself with the popular An Lochan Uaine, the Green Loch.

This route leads from the Hayfield through the forest to the Green Loch and back again. However it is also popular, and shorter, to ski to the Green Loch from Glenmore Lodge. This latter option follows undulating track through more open forest, allowing a greater feel for the steep sides and glacial impact of the Ryvoan Pass.

From the Hayfield go N along the Ski Road to the bridge across the Abhainn Ruigh-eunachan and follow the broad track SE along the N bank of the burn. Cross the burn after 0.5km. There is now a bridge at this point, which has made skiing on these trails far more attractive than in former days when skiers had to ford the waters or seek alternative routes! Continue SE on the good track to a T-junction. Turn E and follow the broad track for 1.5kms, until it meets the Glenmore Lodge - Ryvoan trail. Ski N and follow the Ryvoan trail for 0.5km to the Green Loch.

Return as for the outward route, but for an interesting variation continue straight on at the junction after the bridge over the Allt na Ciste and regain the Ski Road S of the Hayfield via the Allt Mor footbridge. (Note if wishing to find this footbridge from the Ski Road, the trail to it is marked by a ski trail marker post (blue). There are other entrances to the forest between the Hayfield and this trail, but they do not lead directly to the footbridge.)

It is possible to continue from the Green Loch along Route 6 to Ryvoan Bothy and the Abernethy Forest, or to Bynack Stable via Route 14. These routes cross open moorland, where snow cover is not predictable and the weather more noticeable. The tracks are not as smooth and are generally more difficult than those within the forest.

There is a broad forest road leading E then N just N of the footbridge over the Allt Ban. This is a good snow-holding track, skiable with minimum cover. It climbs moderately steeply initially, but then gently giving a good run back down. It is a pretty route, passing the small Lochan na Frithe, and with a trail branching off E along the Allt Ban. Unfortunately it terminates after 1km. There is a path from the end of it, marked on the 1:50,000 OS map, which skiers may have considered as a link with the Ryvoan trail. This is overgrown and difficult to pass along. It holds little snow, and leads to a steep and nasty descent along the edge of the forest to the trail below.

There are also forest roads penetrating the slopes N of Glenmore Lodge which give good skiing for those with basic technique. The tracks terminate at the forest boundary. Continuing beyond this leads onto steep slopes of open forest where advanced techniques would be required for a perilous descent to the Ryvoan Pass.

Skiers may notice red ski trail waymarkers indicating a route running from the "Ski Road" W of the Coire na Ciste car park to the Allt Mor footbridge. This is the "escape route" for storm-bound downhill skiers. It is steep and narrow, and since it may be in use by descending alpine skiers it is not recognised as an ascent route.

There is very pleasant skiing on the moorland above the forest NE of the Coire na Ciste car park, and routes here can be linked to the Ryvoan trail. Skiing is dependent on snow lying below the 550m contour line, but the Allt Ban, and its tributaries are known to hold the snow particularly well. There is a short grass and heather base, and the slopes are gentle. The interesting fluvo-glacial scenery is enhanced by views varied enough to include the Northern Corries, Glen More and Loch Morlich and Ryvoan Pass. Lochan na Beinne is worth a visit. The Allt Ban has incised a trench just before it turns to flow into the forest, but by keeping above this, easy terrain leads through attractive pines to the forest fence. The descent path along the forest edge to the Ryvoan trail is steep and vegetated. It will in most cases be necessary to walk it. Note also the dangers of going N beyond the forest edge onto the steep unsafe slopes below Creag nan Gall. The way down the forest edge is waymarked, although from below the path is only obvious after the first 10m.

10. WHITEWELL TO LOCH AN EILEIN

OS SHEET: 36

START POINT: The tour is described from the road end at Whitewell, GR 915087, but can be started at Blackpark or the Loch an Eilein Car Park. Choice may be determined by how far it is possible to drive along uncleared minor roads, and in deep snow conditions it may be necessary to ski in from Inverdruie. There is a small parking area at Whitewell. At Blackpark parking is by the roadside.

TOTAL DISTANCE: 6.5kms   ASCENT: 90m   TIME: 1 hour 45 minutes

TERRAIN: Broad easy tracks through forest, woods and open moorland. 1.5kms along minor public, but quiet road.

SKIING ABILITIES REQUIRED: Very easy tour. Suitable for beginners.

OTHER ABILITIES REQUIRED: Elementary map reading skills.

SKIING EQUIPMENT NEEDED: Light touring gear.

OTHER EQUIPMENT NEEDED: Lightweight equipment.

SNOW COVER: The land lies between 250m and 300m above sea level. Consequently you need to be opportunistic to be treated to snow along the full length of this tour. Best chances are in the first three months of the year.

APPROACH ROADS: Minor roads, signposted Tullochgrue and Black Park, E of Inverdruie on the Aviemore to Coylumbridge Ski Road.

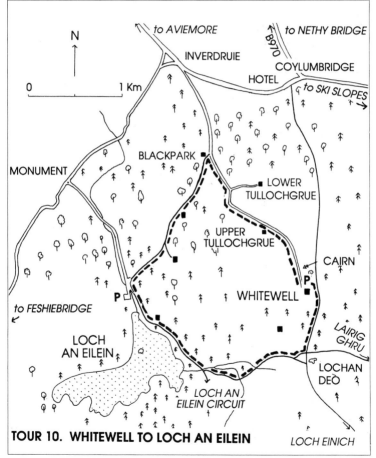

TOUR 10. WHITEWELL TO LOCH AN EILEIN

This is a very beautiful tour, passing in such a short distance through several different types of landscape - open moorland, pine forest, birch wood, loch-side and farmland. It offers stunning views over the Spey Valley to the rolling Monadhliath Hills to the NW and the grand Cairngorms to the SE. It is a sheltered alternative when high winds rule out any touring on the High Tops.

The tour can be skied in either direction. It is described here in a clockwise direction. This way the slope at Tullochgrue is ascended rather than descended, which beginners will appreciate. The descent of this section needs some downhill skill! The clockwise course also gives a very steady downhill advantage over 75% of the route!

Leave the road end to go E across the open moorland (footpath signposted), bypassing a cairn erected here to the memory of two climbers who lost their lives in these hills in 1928, and reach quickly the main track from Coylumbridge. Follow this due S until a major junction of paths is reached by the site of a pond. Low signposts tucked neatly by the trees indicate the routes to Coylumbridge, Loch Einich, Lairig Ghru and Loch an Eilein. It is the latter track leading W over moorland which our route follows. There are two streams to cross, but otherwise no problems, just beautiful views, and glimpses of the loch ahead.

At the junction turn right (signposted Aviemore) and follow the broad track which is part of the popular trail around Loch an Eilein, where the delightful forest and views of the loch distract from the effort of an uphill haul. At the end of the loch do not cross the stream, but continue to the public road. Go along this for only 50 yards, and then take the track leading off to the right. The skiing is wonderfully easy along a broad, almost flat track, through open fields and birch woods.

Finally upon reaching the house and road at Blackpark turn right and return to Whitewell along the road, (this may have been cleared). The road climbs steadily through birch woods and then open moor and offers panoramic views of the Cairngorms ahead, with Aviemore intruding behind. The loch to the N is Loch Pityoulish.

11. GLEANN EINICH

OS SHEET: 36

START POINT: The route is described from the road end at Whitewell, GR 915087, where there is a small parking area. It is also possible to begin from Coylumbridge, GR 914107 (roadside parking), or along Route 10 from Loch an Eilein car park, GR 897086 (fee payable).

TOTAL DISTANCE: 20kms   ASCENT: 200m   TIME: 5 hours 20 minutes

TERRAIN: Good track along the floor of the glen. Crossing the Beanaidh Bheag can be a problem if it is not frozen.

SKIING ABILITIES REQUIRED: Easy track requiring basic technique only. If skiing as far as the loch - ability to cover the distance.

OTHER ABILITIES REQUIRED: Elementary map reading skills.

SKIING EQUIPMENT NEEDED: Light touring gear.

OTHER EQUIPMENT NEEDED: Lightweight equipment.

SNOW COVER: Requires snow at 300m. Does not have good snow holding properties. Often cover is thin and intermittent when it is complete in Glen More Forest.

APPROACH ROADS: B970 Inverdruie to Coylumbridge. Minor road S at Inverdruie to Blackpark and Whitewell.

Given the fortunate occurrence of a snow fall in the glens this route gives some good track skiing into remote and wild scenery, a welcome gasp of tree-free air, not available along the more popular forest trails nearby. But note, the lack of timber also brings two disadvantages. Snow cover is not as good or as well preserved as in the forest, and the weather is not kept out. Consequently common snow conditions greeting the skier are poor - slush or ice with bare patches. From time to time, however, the ideal conditions do occur and the track skier can glide effortlessly to the peaceful loneliness of Loch Einich, securely entrenched below Braeriach's Cairngorm magnificence and the savage buttresses of Sgor Gaoith and Sgoran Dubh Mor.

Follow Route 10 to the junction of tracks, GR 916079 by Lochan Deo. The Gleann Einich track is signposted, and leads SE, skirting

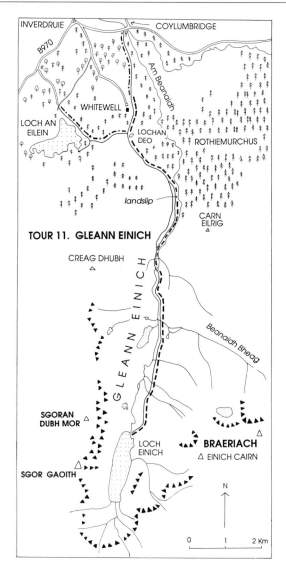

INVERDRUIE   COYLUMBRIDGE

B970

Am Beanaidh

WHITEWELL

LOCH AN
EILEIN

LOCHAN
DEO   ROTHIEMURCHUS

landslip

CARN
EILRIG
△

TOUR 11. GLEANN EINICH

CREAG DHUBH
△

GLEANN EINICH

Beanaidh Bheag

SGORAN
DUBH MOR △

LOCH
EINICH

BRAERIACH

△ EINICH CAIRN

SGOR GAOITH △

N

0   1   2 Km

pine woods and ascending gradually to meet the Am Beanaidh. The track then runs S along the floor of the glen eventually reaching Loch Einich. This is the terminus. Return back down the track.

For the effort there is reward in the scenery - compulsory river scenery where the track and the Am Beanaidh snake together, towards a stark backdrop of mountains ripped apart by glaciers. There are unique views of Braeriach's NW facing corries.

The Beanaidh Bheag can be difficult to cross, and some skiers are thwarted at this barrier. Sadly for them, they miss out the most impressive scenery at the head of the glen. Otherwise there are no difficulties, weather permitting, although skiers might note that some landslip has occurred and destroyed a short stretch of track above the Am Beanaidh in Grid Square 9206.

12. THE CORRIES OF CAIRN GORM

OS SHEET: 36

The Corries of Cairn Gorm are a playground for cross-country skiers. The Northern Corries have the ideal criteria for snow accumulation and storage - high altitude (above 650m), N facing aspect and high cliffs shading them from the sun and trapping the snow. They have been skied from November through to June and offer all types of terrain from the flat to the very exciting! They are accessible and give sheltered skiing when the plateau is inhospitable. The Southern Corries offer skiing at around 1000m, enjoy a long season and again have a variety of gradients, including those suited to beginners, but are more remote especially if the skier prefers not to use the uplift facilities provided for downhill skiers.

Mountain skiing gear is required for any trip to the corries, and dress and supplies should be appropriate to deal with the worst of British mountain weather. Navigation in the Northern Corries is not too critical, as in poor visibility skiing downhill will lead to the safety of Glen More, but in the Southern Corries route finding must be accurate.

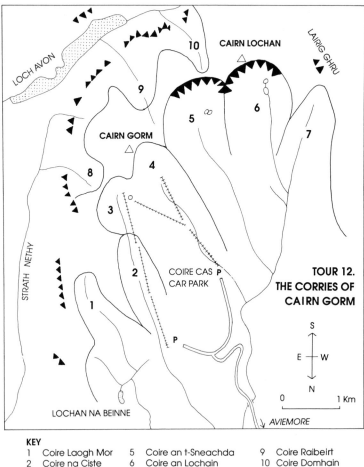

TOUR 12.
THE CORRIES OF
CAIRN GORM

KEY

1	Coire Laogh Mor	5	Coire an t-Sneachda	9	Coire Raibeirt
2	Coire na Ciste	6	Coire an Lochain	10	Coire Domhain
3	Ptarmigan Bowl	7	Lurcher's Gully		
4	Coire Cas	8	Ciste Mhearad		

NORTHERN CORRIES

1. Coire Laogh Mor

This is the most northerly of Cairn Gorm's corries, accessed from the Coire na Ciste car park. It holds snow well, but is steep in its upper section and since it is not as scenically dramatic as the other corries, it does not receive much attention. There is good skiing in the lower reaches and towards and below Lochan na Beinne. Snow holds well along the tributary of the Allt Ban flowing NE from the car park where the skiing is sheltered. There is also good skiing above the steep section of the corrie along the ridge radiating N from Cnap Coire na Spreidhe. Skiing above Strath Nethy has been favourably compared with skiing above the Lairig Ghru.

2. Coire na Ciste

Coire na Ciste has been developed with uplift facilities for the downhill skier. It has a car park, café and toilet facilities and there are lots of people! The upper part of the corrie can be accessed from the Ptarmigan Restaurant. The runs are steep and narrow in places, prone to mogulling, and littered with downhill skiers. The "West Wall" and the "East Wall" of the corrie are downhill runs of popularity, but often icy and not for the beginner, faint-hearted or squeamish.

3. Ptarmigan Bowl

This is the area to the E of the Ptarmigan Restaurant, and is in fact the upper section of the Coire na Ciste. The bowl holds snow well, even when elsewhere there is none, and often patches can be found here in summer. A broad expanse with easy gradient, it is ideal for beginners and learning downhill techniques on. It is served by drag tows, but appears less crowded than other pistes because of the large area available. It is recommendable to ski here in the evenings of late season when the tows have closed. Several hours of practice on pisted, easy snow can thus be enjoyed in eerie tranquillity.

4. Coire Cas

Coire Cas is crammed with uplift facilities for downhill skiers. It has excellent snow holding capabilities, which have been enhanced by snow fencing. It offers a variety of gradients for cross-country downhill including the extremely steep ski run down the headwall, and the famous "White Lady" Piste, usually mogulled. Both have been skied on skinny skis. There are also easy traverses, and nursery slopes below the White Lady Shieling half-way station.

5. Coire an t-Sneachda

Aptly named "Coire of the Snows", this corrie is approached by skiing 1km SW from the Coire Cas car park. It stores large snowfields and often even as late as May there is no need to go too far to find a practice area. The gradients are generally gentle and ideal for beginners. This is a corrie of great serenity and majestic cliff-line scenery - at the moment still a haven of peacefulness - although threatened by invasion for downhill skiing.

It is only 3kms and 300m of climbing from the car park to the beautiful head of Coire an t-Sneachda.

6. Coire an Lochain

Kin of Coire an t-Sneachda, but less frequented by cross-country skiers, probably as it is farther from the car park and cannot offer any snowfields not available in the nearer corrie. Indeed in the upper reaches the corrie floor is boulder-strewn and almost flat. However the cliff-line scenery is worth a visit (3.5kms and 300m climbing from the Coire Cas car park). The bothy known as Jeans Hut was sited in Coire an Lochain, but was removed in 1986 as it was becoming unfeasible to maintain it. Note the Great Slab at the head of the corrie which avalanches reliably every year.

7. Lurcher's Gully

This is the home of the Allt Creag an Leth-choin - the Lurcher's Burn. It is an excellent snow-holding gully, and as it is visible from the "Ski Road" its snow cover can be checked before deciding to visit it. The gully will test a beginner, but the sides are not too uncomfortable natural buffers. In its upper reaches the gradient eases into a broad flat col - Lurcher's Meadow - an ideal practice zone. The view from Lurcher's Meadow across the Lairig Ghru is quite spectacular. Braeriach's massive form hides The Angel's Peak and Cairn Toul, but The Devil's Point sneaks into view to the S. To the W Sgor Gaoith's cliff-lined flank plunges to Loch Einich, whilst beyond the Monadhliath Hills fade gently away to the distant Creag Meagaidh range. Be wary in mist of the steep drop into the Lairig Ghru on the far side of Lurcher's Meadow.

Lurcher's Gully offers the cross-country skier a quiet and easy angled route to the High Tops, and the easiest descent from the plateau. The ski run is a favourite of many.

Even in late season or sparse snow cover the traverse across the moor between the Coire Cas car park and Lurcher's Gully can usually be skied for most of the way along a ribbon of snow which lingers in a peaty depression below the path. This can be seen and checked from the Ski Road.

SOUTHERN CORRIES

8. Ciste Mhearad

Less than 1km skiing SE from the Ptarmigan Restaurant takes the skier to the peace of Ciste Mhearad. This bowl on the NE flank of Cairn Gorm is well noted for its snow holding properties, and is one place to look for snow if you wish to ski at midsummer! Snow has even been known to remain throughout the summer and when snow disappeared from here in 1969 it was for the first time since 1959. Snow depths of 20m have been recorded.

The descent into the bowl may be quite daunting for the less able, but the slope eases, to give a run out. However, straying too far down the bowl will eventually lead to steep slopes that are daunting to non-beginners too, as the land plunges to become Strath Nethy!

9. Coire Raibeirt

Hanging above Loch Avon and strung on the S flank of Cairn Gorm this corrie offers easy slopes in its upper bowl and fine views of Ben Macdui and Beinn Mheadhoin. Interesting and pleasant, but really on the wrong side of the hill to gain popularity. It steepens dramatically towards Loch Avon in the lower section - to give a difficult but exhilarating run in good conditions for those competent descending steep slopes.

Loch Avon is sometimes frozen and skiable. If so, and the skier is sure of the safety of the ice, this corrie gives a good route to reach the usually more remote terrain beyond Loch Avon.

10. Coire Domhain

Between Cairn Lochan and Coire Raibeirt, this corrie also offers easy sheltered slopes and fine views. It tends to hold the snow better than Coire Raibeirt, and is crossed on the "trade route" from Cairn Gorm to Ben Macdui. It can be a good bet in the early months and may still be holding some snow in early summer. Again, be wary of the sudden plunge steeply down to Loch Avon in the lower reaches of the corrie.

A popular route suitable for short days leads from the summit of Cairn Gorm above the cliffs of Coire an t-Sneachda and Coire an Lochain to Cairn Lochan, returning to the Coire Cas car park via Lurcher's Gully. This is a straightforward route in ideal conditions, but potentially a serious undertaking in poor visibility (when there is little point in doing it anyway).

13. BEN MACDUI

OS SHEET: 36   START POINT: Coire Cas Car Park, GR 989062

TOTAL DISTANCE: 17kms   ASCENT: 821m

TIME: 5 hours 30 minutes not using lifts.

TERRAIN: Stony ridge leading to open tundra plateau, descent down snow-filled gully and across heather moor.

SKIING ABILITIES REQUIRED: Good basic skills of climbing, traverse and snow plough, but if ascending Fiacaill a' Choire Chais skill in ascending steep, often icy and stony ground also necessary. Ability to cope with different snow conditions.

OTHER ABILITIES REQUIRED: Excellent winter navigation and hillcraft skills. Good general fitness.

SKIING EQUIPMENT NEEDED: Mountain touring gear. Skins if ascending Fiacaill a' Choire Chais on skis.

OTHER EQUIPMENT NEEDED: Full mountain equipment. Crampons for Fiacaill a' Choire Chais.

SNOW COVER: Excellent. High altitude, and N facing aspects ensure a very long season - the longest in Britain. Some skiing is often possible from November to June. Parts of the plateau prone to blowing clear especially in early season or prolonged strong winds.

APPROACH ROADS: "Ski Road" from Aviemore.

This tour is one of the most popular of all ski tours in Scotland. Indeed it has become a "classic". The tour can be undertaken by those with basic skiing skills, the plateau is skiable for up to six months of the year, the scenery is magnificent, the views spectacular and the descent sheer fun. However this is all on a good day. The schizophrenical plateau is also well known for its cruel weather, and is no place to be in bad conditions. The summit is remote, and although the skiing is straightforward, perfect navigation is required to avoid the steep cliffs of the Lairig Ghru, the Northern Corries and at the head of Loch Avon.

From the car park ski/walk to the White Lady Shieling half-way station of the downhill pistes, and cut across Coire Cas onto the steep ridge - Fiacaill a' Choire Chais. This may be blown clear, and

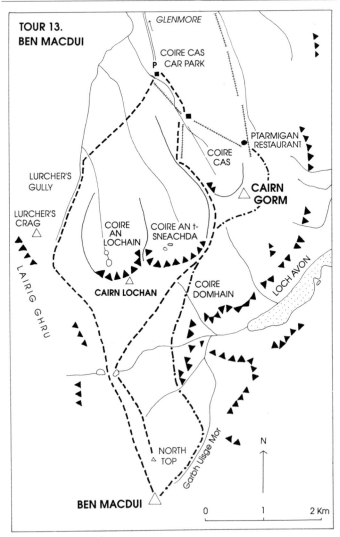

TOUR 13.
BEN MACDUI

treacherously icy, with cornices on the lee side. Take care and walk if in doubt. From the cairn at the top of the ridge (height 1141m) ski S, away from the beast of Cairn Gorm itself following along the top of the Coire an t-Sneachda cliff-line. When the slope leading up to Cairn Lochan is reached turn SW and traverse above Coire Domhain to the flat area of the Lochan Buidhe. From here the final ascent is launched up broad slopes, firstly to the lower "North" Top and from there a final 0.5km to the main summit.

On a clear day the summit is a fine viewpoint and it is fun to identify distant mountains with the help of the information plaque by the summit cairn. Until 1810 Ben Macdui was thought to be the highest mountain in Britain. In fact it is the second highest. However nowhere in the country is such a high level maintained over such a wide area (7 square kilometres above 1100m). It is the king of Scottish mountains to the Nordic skier. In fact, if the Cairngorms had not been so rudely interrupted by the Ice Age, the Lairig Ghru would not have been scooped out by glaciers and a plateau of delightful enormity would today exist between Ben Macdui and Baeriach. As it is, the kin are separated, but the Braeriach plateau (5 square kilometres above 1100m) is a worthy sibling to that of Ben Macdui.

Return to the March Burn Lochan safely at speed over the broad uncomplicated N flank. After ascending approximately 50m from here towards Cairn Lochan, a descending traverse keeping well above the steep and cliff-marked slope of the Lairig Ghru leads down to and over the flat alp marked 1083m on the Ordnance Survey map, and on down again to the broad col known as Lurcher's Meadow. From here the descent to the car park down Lurcher's Gully is a super downhill run and a favourite of many cross-country skiers. The final traverse across the peat and heather moor to the car park can be skied quite late in the season by joining ribbons of snow which linger here, despite the disappearance of snow elsewhere.

Alternatives

1. If you wish to use the chair-lift to gain speedy access to the plateau the best route from the Ptarmigan Restaurant to rejoin the tour described above is to ski to the top of the drag lifts above the Ptarmigan Bowl and traverse around the E flank of Cairn Gorm. Here there is better snow cover, less ascent, and an easier gradient to

traverse in descent rather than the busy trade route over Cairn Gorm summit, which is often blown clear and a mishmash of stones and ice.

2. The descent down the Garbh Uisge Mor is a cracker and although it will test a beginner it can be descended with basic skills. From the summit of Ben Macdui ski NE and follow the route of the burn to the site of two small lochans. Do not descend below these, but turn NNW and traverse above the cliffs at the head of Loch Avon, to the Feith Buidhe. The run from the summit is usually skiable to this point at midsummer. Either ascend NW to join the route to Lurcher's Gully or cut across Coire Domhain to head back to Cairn Gorm.

14. BYNACK MORE

OS SHEET: 36

START POINT: Road end beyond Glenmore Lodge, GR 989095

TOTAL DISTANCE: 24kms   ASCENT: 750m   TIME: 7 hours 15 minutes

TERRAIN: Land-Rover track, leading to heather moorland. Both steep slopes and broad plateau.

SKIING ABILITIES REQUIRED: Ability to negotiate steep, but broad slopes, and cross deep heather - step turns being recommended for the latter.

OTHER ABILITIES REQUIRED: Good winter navigation and hillcraft skills. General fitness.

SKIING EQUIPMENT NEEDED: Mountain touring gear.

OTHER EQUIPMENT NEEDED: Full mountain equipment.

SNOW COVER: The initial tracks require snow below 350m - but only a light covering is necessary to ski them. The plateaux collect the snow and hold it, but the deep heather in places demands a good accumulation to ensure enjoyable passage!

APPROACH ROADS: "Ski Road" from Aviemore. Shortly after Glenmore Youth Hostel take the track left up to and past Glenmore Lodge Training Centre.

This is a pleasantly mixed tour of track, moor and mountain skiing leading to a fine viewpoint.

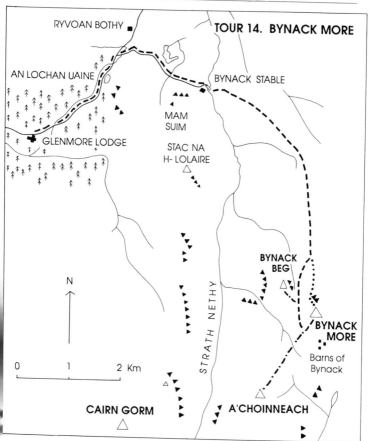

Take the track through the glacially incised Ryvoan Pass, and bear left 0.5kms after An Lochan Uaine along an easy track across open moor to the corrugated iron hut - Bynack Stable. Cross the Nethy (bridge) and thrust energetically up the shoulder domineering to the SE gaining height rapidly (path to follow if snow cover is poor). The next 2kms are across open plateaux, with only gentle ascent, and where, if the snow is deep, skiers become the envy of walkers.

Walkers however will choose to climb Bynack More directly up the very steep N ridge. Skiers are better advised to either discard skis before this steep gradient and also ascend on foot, or to traverse SW into the coire of the Allt a' Choire Dhuibh, and ascend to the col between Bynack Beg and Bynack More. From here a leisurely ascending traverse around the mountain leads to the S shoulder and a gentle approach to the summit.

The rocky knobs passed on the ridge are the little Barns of Bynack. They are granite tors. Larger examples - the Barns of Bynack themselves - are found on the E of this ridge at GR 045058. They are worthy of a visit, although be wary in mist of the very steep gradient of the slope below them.

From Bynack More there is an unusual rewarding view of the Cairngorm Mountains rising majestically above the deep troughs of Strath Nethy and Loch Avon.

Return by the route of ascent, but first consider the addition of A' Choinneach to the day's itinerary. This Munro Top lies SW of the main summit, and its inclusion adds only 2kms and 80m of ascent to the day's journey. This is easy skiing and a must if the Cairngorms are in view. Similarly, Bynack Beg can be bagged in ten minutes from the col separating it from the main summit.

It is possible to follow the Allt a' Choire Dhuibh and return to Bynack Stable via Strath Nethy. However, the descent is steep in parts requiring skilled skiing, and Strath Nethy can be a boggy struggle. Far nicer to make use of the tracks you made in ascent, and the 2kms easy downhill across the plateau are a joy. The shoulder down to Bynack Stable requires a repertoire of techniques if snow cover is thin and the heather is trying to embrace your skis.

THE EASTERN CAIRNGORMS

The massive area of high ground E of Glen Derry and S of Glen Avon boasts some of the best Nordic touring terrain in the country. Here lie the Eastern Cairngorms, including Ben Avon and Beinn a' Bhuird, two mountains grand enough to be associated with Cairn Gorm, Ben Macdui, Braeriach and Cairn Toul in the Cairngorm "Six Tops" grouping. Here also is the Moine Bhealaidh (the Broom Moss or the Yellow Moss) an expanse of box and turf above the 800m contour line, which under snow gives more skiing on level ground than might ever be enjoyed at lower levels. Beinn a' Chaorainn to the N of the Moss and Beinn Bhreac at its southern edge are both Munro Summits and have approaches and runs well suited to Nordic skis.

Certainly the attraction to skiers here is the vast plateau areas with their snow-holding properties allowing long routes across easy slopes. However there is some excellent downhill running too, along the numerous burns radiating in all directions from the plateau snowfield. The run from the N Top of Beinn a' Bhuird SW along the Allt Coire Ruairidh and then via the Dubh-Ghleann to Glen Quoich was once rated as the longest schuss in the country. Slesser (1970) describes the SE corrie of Beinn a' Bhuird as the finest open skiing in Scotland. The plateau has been sculptured by glaciers and dissected by water to such an extent, that although it rises steeply, slopes of all gradients have been created along its edges, and routes exist for the extreme or the average skier.

This area enjoys a very fortunate position with regard to snow accumulation. Situated in the E of the country it is well-placed to receive the snow-bearing easterlies. Yet it is protected from the thawing warm south-westerlies by the huge Cairngorm landmass to the W. This landmass forces air moving from the W to rise and cool, so that by the time it reaches Glen Derry it is colder than it was at the River Spey. Consequently early falls of snow on the more westerly Cairngorm heights are sometimes removed by a thawing south-westerly, but such falls of snow on the hills E of Glen Derry escape such a fate.

This is one of the largest areas in the country at this height, and although sea level temperatures may reach 8 or 10 degrees centigrade it could still be cold enough for precipitation to fall as snow on the plateau. An ideal base of moss, heath and grass means skiing is possible with minimum snow cover. The chance of some early skiing combined with lingering snow late in the season gives this area one of the longest seasons for ski touring in Britain.

Despite the above attractions for skiers the area is not frequently visited. Many are deterred by the inaccessibility of these hills which lie away from population centres, and are not penetrated by roads. However there are some very useful Land-Rover tracks which will take the explorer into the area, made all the more attractive by its very remoteness.

There are a number of approach routes used. These pass through some outstanding natural pine forest and glen scenery and are worthy in their own rights not just as a means to the skiing grounds. From the S, Glen Derry is often used to reach Beinn Bhreac, the Yellow Moss, and Beinn a' Chaorainn. The track up Glen Quoich continues up An Diollaid and so to Beinn a' Bhuird. Gleann an t-Slugain offers a route from Invercauld to the ruined Slugan Lodge and hence to The Sneck up the upper reaches of the Quoich Water. A track going N from Invercauld to Loch Builg gives a long approach, but after snowfall can be skied for much of the way and links with the runs on the SE slopes of Ben Avon. From the N, Ben Avon is approached from Inchrory, which is served by good tracks to Tomintoul in the N, and the A939 at Cock Bridge in the E. An estate road up Glen Gairn leads to Loch Builg and is a useful escape from the snow-retaining runs on the E slopes of Ben Avon.

15. BEINN A' BHUIRD

OS SHEETS: 43 and 36

START POINT: End of public road by Linn of Quoich, GR 117911

TOTAL DISTANCE: 27kms   ASCENT: 920m   TIME: 8 hours 15 minutes

TERRAIN: Land-Rover track leading from sheltered glen to exposed high level plateau. Descent down snow-filled burn, steepening in its middle section.

SKIING ABILITIES REQUIRED: Basic ascent and traverse skills. Ability to descend steep section of burn. Ability to ski the distance.

OTHER ABILITIES REQUIRED: Excellent winter navigation and hillcraft skills.

SKIING EQUIPMENT NEEDED: Mountain touring gear.

OTHER EQUIPMENT NEEDED: Full mountain equipment.

SNOW COVER: Excellent at upper heights, but to ski the whole route requires snow lying above 300m. Track prone to drifting and snow may linger on it. Snow cover particularly good along Allt an t-Sneachda, usually lasting well into spring.

APPROACH ROADS: Minor public road W of Braemar via Linn of Dee. Parking E of bridge over Quoich Water.

Since half of this tour lies in the glen the winter months hold the most promise for those attracted by skiing the whole route. Spring, however, is also a good time, for this is a challenging route, best done when days are longer and the weather less stormy. Snow will still be lying on Beinn a' Bhuird, Britain's tenth highest mountain, after the winter snows have left lower hills.

Much of the route is on estate tracks, which ascend almost to the summit plateau. These may annoy some skiers. Certainly their existence spoils the natural scenery and remoteness of the area. However, they speed progress on a lengthy route and can provide a useful ribbon of snow in lean times, for snow collects and lingers on them.

Although the approach through the glen is long, it is an attractive place to ski, and the open pine and birch wood and river scenery

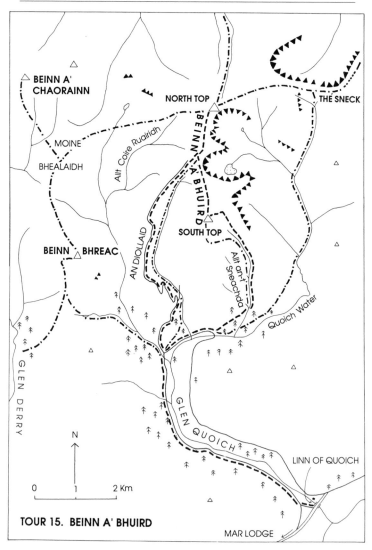

TOUR 15. BEINN A' BHUIRD

contrasts with the high plateau and plunging corries of the mountain ahead.

The route follows the track on the SW side of Quoich Water, continuing N along the track as it ascends An Diollaid, a broad-nosed ridge radiating S from Beinn a' Bhuird. Crossing the waters descending from the Dubh-Ghleann may be a problem as there is no bridge. Steady climbing up the track leads to a broadening of the ridge and an easing of the gradient as the summit plateau is approached. The ridge may be icy - a feature of its S-facing aspect. Once on the plateau there are extensive views to Lochnagar and the main Cairngorm massif, but more immediately down to the impressive craggy corries cut into the E face of the mountain. The cliffs carry huge cornices and the drop is quite sudden compared with the gentle shelving of the tableland to the W. Beinn a' Bhuird's North Top, the highest point, is reached by easy skiing N across the plateau. It is marked by a small cairn.

Return along the plateau to the South Top - an easy romp in clear conditions, but requiring precise route finding in mist.

The route of descent to Glen Quoich follows the Allt an t-Sneachda. This is a long and superb descent, one of the best in the Cairngorms, leading to delightful open pine woods. There is usually snow lying in the burn well into the spring. Heading directly to the burn from the South Top leads down a steep slope SE of the summit. This can be avoided by first skiing due S and then traversing E to the burn, or by skiing ENE before heading S. In the latter case care should be taken to keep well W of the rock buttresses and crags to the E.

From the pine woods return W along the N bank of Quoich Water to the open flats below An Diollaid and the outward route, which is then retraced to the start point.

Alternatives from the North Top of Beinn a' Bhuird

1. The Moine Bhealaidh

A longer route back via the Moine Bhealaidh and Beinn Bhreac leads across excellent langlauf terrain of broad easy slopes and flat moss. The run from the North Top SW down the upper reaches of the Allt Coire Ruairidh and then W across the Moss is particularly satisfying. Adam Watson described this two-mile descent as the best run of the day in his report of his historic traverse of the Cairngorm "Six Tops" on langlauf skis in April 1962. In mist it is necessary to check bearings on this section, for it is easy to follow the descending slope into Coire Ruairidh in Glen Avon instead of the Coire Ruairidh of Dubh-Ghleann. The Glen Avon Coire Ruairidh is an excellent snow holding burn, a handy receptacle for snow blown by prevailing westerlies from the Moine Bhealaidh. However, despite its qualities it leads to remote country.

From the Moine Bhealaidh there are no difficulties ascending the Munro Summit of Beinn Bhreac. Easy slopes descend S from the shallow col W of the summit, from where return can be made to the track in Glen Derry or via Poll Bhat to that in Glen Quoich.

2. Alltan na Beinne

To return from the summit plateau to Glen Quoich via the Alltan na Beinne involves skiing a steep and narrow section, although above and below this there are long runs on easy slopes. For those with competent descent skills this is a satisfying route, for snow lingers well here - usually into spring. The burn is prone to cornicing.

3. Descending N from the North Top

The runs N from the summit plateau are among the best langlauf descents in the country. Unfortunately they lead away from civilisation, which makes them unpopular, but pleasantly quiet for the enthusiasts who do venture along them. A N-facing aspect, and good positioning to receive wind-blown snow from the higher ground means they have a generous snow rating. Of particular note is the run due N from the summit along the Feith Ghiubhasachain. This is over 5kms in length, and descends broad, gentle slopes to reach the River Avon at a height of 540m above sea level. There is a bridge across the River Avon, just upstream of the confluence. It may be difficult to locate in deep snow.

4. To Ben Avon via The Sneck

From the North Top of Beinn a' Bhuird easy plateau skiing leads to Ben Avon further E - that is with the exception of where the plateau has been eroded at The Sneck. Here the plateau descends to below the significant 1000m contour line, and the cliffs of Garbh Choire and upper Slochd Mor lie immediately N. The Sneck is skiable in good conditions, but due care and good skiing abilities are required. It may be necessary to use crampons, not skis, on this section. Accurate navigation is required between the two summits. The plateau is extensive and featureless with the exception of the tors or barns, which all appear similar in mist and may actually add to confusion.

From The Sneck it is possible to return to Glen Quoich by descending due S along the upper reaches of Quoich Water, a long and interesting run allowing some insight into the spectacular E face of Beinn a' Bhuird.

16. BEN AVON

OS SHEETS: 36

START POINT: Car park, GR 165176. (Road up Glen Avon is private, with a locked gate at Birchfield, GR 167148.)

TOTAL DISTANCE: 42kms   ASCENT: 850m   TIME: 12 hours

TERRAIN: Long approach on metalled road. Broad ridge ascending to extensive open plateau, mainly grassy. Descent down snow-filled burn steepening in its middle section. Slopes of all gradients.

SKIING ABILITIES REQUIRED: Ability to ski mountain slopes of all gradients. Ability to ski the distance.

OTHER ABILITIES REQUIRED: Excellent winter navigation and hillcraft skills and good general fitness.

SKIING EQUIPMENT NEEDED: Mountain touring gear.

OTHER EQUIPMENT NEEDED: Full mountain equipment.

SNOW COVER: Excellent on the mountain itself and in the descent burn, lasting well into spring. Some of the approach may be skiable - but this is dependent on snow lying at 350m.

APPROACH ROADS: Minor road from Tomintoul leading SW to River Avon.

The mountain massif of Ben Avon can hardly be ignored as a skier's mountain. The extensive plateau gives several kilometres of skiing above the 1000m contour line across excellent langlauf terrain. The many ridges radiating in all directions from its heights are separated by snow-trapping corries and burns, where slopes of all gradients

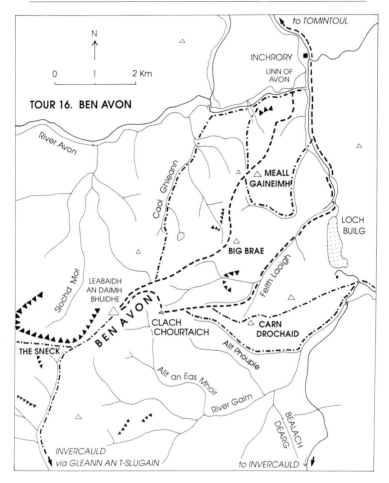

TOUR 16. BEN AVON

to TOMINTOUL

N

0   1   2 Km

INCHRORY

LINN OF AVON

River Avon

Caol Ghleann

MEALL GAINEIMH

LOCH BUILG

BIG BRAE

Feith Laoigh

Slochd Mor

LEABAIDH AN DAIMH BHUIDHE

BEN AVON

CLACH CHOURTAICH

CARN DROCHAID

THE SNECK

Allt Phouple

Allt an Eas Mhoir

River Gairn

BEALACH DEARG

INVERCAULD via GLEANN AN T-SLUGAIN

to INVERCAULD

have been eroded to give long and exhilarating ski runs. It blocks the passage of snow-bearing NE winds, and holds the snow well in its scooped and dissected flanks. If skied with Beinn a' Bhuird it is a classic high level ski tour. In recent years it has become fashionable to ski the "Six Tops" of the Cairngorms (Cairn Gorm, Ben Macdui, Braeriach, Cairn Toul, Beinn a' Bhuird and Ben Avon). Ben Avon is the lowest of these six mountains, but it can hardly be regarded as the little sister, for it boasts ten "tops" over 3,000 feet (Munro summit, tops and deleted tops) and 8 square kilometres above the 1000m contour line.

The joys of skiing here are however reserved for the fit, enthusiastic or devoted. Ben Avon can only be accessed by long approaches from distant roads and if the skier is alarmed at the 11km trek from the start point of this tour to the foot of the mountain he will be dismayed to find no magical short cuts. This is a long day, although by strapping skis to a bicycle the approach can be accelerated. The track to Inchrory gives a reasonable cycling surface, although until April it may well be snow-covered in places. Once at the foot of the mountain the summit still lies 8kms away over terrain where even in clear visibility the map should be constantly checked to follow the best route. In mist route finding can be confusing.

From the car park above the River Avon follow the broad track S along the E side of the river. The track ascends gradually up the glen to Inchrory, continuing S for 1km before crossing the Builg Burn (bridge) and then heading W beyond the picturesque Linn of Avon.

The summer walkers' route from Linn of Avon ascends the ridge to the col W of Meall Gaineimh. This is a reasonable ski ascent - especially if using skins - but if snow cover on the ridge appears poor from below it may well be worth following the Land-Rover track W for a further kilometre and searching out better snow cover in the burn descending from the col between Meall Gaineimh and Clach Bhan. Clach Bhan is a most intriguing tor displaying scooped pot-holes created by wind-whipped water and scouring debris. From the col the route continues SW, ascending to Big Brae via the E flank of East Meur Gorm Craig. 3.5kms of easy skiing up broad, gentle slopes lead to the huge summit tor of the mountain.

The summit plateau allows extensive views over surrounding sprawling and desolate moors and the former draining pattern of the area, when the River Avon flowed into the River Don instead of the

River Spey as at present, becomes topographically apparent.

From the summit there are numerous descents (see below), including returning via the route of ascent to the track at Linn of Avon. However a long and interesting run using mostly easy slopes descends the snow-holding E flank of the mountain to Glen Builg via the Feith Laoigh. However, it is strongly stressed that great care should be taken on this route to avoid following the easy ski run descending E along the burn which falls over crags at GR 159025. Avoid this danger by starting the descent at Clach Choutsaich, traversing due E to gain the burn which also flows E, but keeps well S of the crags. The burn descends to peat hags and more gentle slopes. The Feith Laoigh has eroded a gorge in its final descent to join the Builg Burn N of Loch Builg, but it is possible to ski above this on its S flank to reach the glen. Inchrory lies 4kms to the N and can be quickly reached along the Land-Rover track descending Glen Builg.

Alternative Approaches

1. From the E via Glen Gairn

An estate road up Glen Gairn gives an alternative approach to the snow-holding E flanks of Ben Avon. Once again a bicycle can be used to speed progress to the mountain. From the glen the route ascends to the col between Carn Drochaid and Carn Dearg and then via Clach Choutsaich to the summit plateau. This route involves some climbing of steep slopes especially above Carn Drochaid - for which skins are recommended.

2. From the S via Gleann an t-Slugain

From the River Dee at Invercauld Bridge this route leads to Ben Avon via Gleann an t-Slugain and the upper reaches of Quoich Water approaching the summit plateau from The Sneck. It is a long approach, but with the exception of the steep section E of The Sneck, the slopes are generally easy-angled. This route allows a look at the spectacular E face of Beinn a' Bhuird.

Alternative Descents

1. To the N

There are numerous descents heading N from the summit plateau, each giving a long schuss into snow-holding terrain. However they all include steep sections requiring competent descent skills. There are steep, avalanche-prone slopes above the descent burns. Generally speaking, these are runs for those with experience, skill and judgement. The descent of Caol Ghleann is particularly noteworthy. This is a known snow-trap giving a long and pleasing run from the plateau to the River Avon. It appears easy at first, but steepens before opening out to more gentle slopes again.

2. To the E and SE

The E and SE flanks of Ben Avon collect and hold the snow and have been greatly dissected by burns to give numerous descents to Glen Builg and Glen Gairn. Once again most of these have steep sections, but give great sport to the competent skier. Indeed, although it is inadvisable to attempt to ski those runs of the upper Feith Laoigh which fall over cliffs S of Big Brae, the waterfall here has been considered by skisters of the past. The Allt Gaineimh curving around Meall Gaineimh, the N outlier of Ben Avon, and descending to Glen Builg traps the snow and gives skiing on mostly reasonable gradients. Other popular descents on this side of the hill are along the courses of the Allt Phouple and the Allt an Eas Mhoir. For those descending in this direction an escape route to the civilisation of Deeside can be sought via the Bealach Dearg which links with the track between Invercauld and Loch Builg. In snowy years the track may be skiable for much of the return.

THE GREAT MOSS

The Moine Mhor or Great Moss is a vast tract of plateau making up the W section of the Cairngorm mountain range. The plateau lies predominantly above the 800m contour line and consequently receives a generous helping of snow each year, which is then well-preserved in the sub-Arctic climate. The tundra vegetation gives an ideal base to the snow and the easy and manageable gradients of the undulating terrain mean that this area of vast snow fields is one of the most important Nordic touring areas in the British Isles.

A choice of well-define tracks assist skiers to ascend to the plateau, whilst the return to the glens is enhanced by a series of favourite runs along snow-holding burns.

However, anyone considering an outing here should be well prepared for the harsh climate and the remoteness of the area, and be aware of the sudden steep plunging cliffs along the margins of much of the plateau. Navigational problems are many. There are few points of reference, there is likely to be poor visibility, and even the usual trustworthy slope angle and distance measures cannot be relied upon here. Watercourses, tracks and cairns may be buried.

Snow conditions on the Great Moss are variable. However it is worth noting that snow lies long here, and so will have been bashed about and redistributed by the wind, melted by the sun and refrozen again. Sastrugi, cornices on cliffs and along courses of burns, alternating patches of ice and soft snow are common.

17. MONADH MOR

OS SHEET: 36 OR 43   START POINT: End of public road, GR 852976
TOTAL DISTANCE: 20kms   ASCENT: 1070m   TIME: 6 hours 50 minutes

TERRAIN: Good path ascending to gently undulating tundra plateau, rising to broad summit ridge. Descent down snow-filled burn.

SKIING ABILITIES REQUIRED: Ability to ascend steep track and cover long distances. Traverse and kick turn, and snowplough at least for the descent.

OTHER ABILITIES REQUIRED: Excellent winter navigation and hillcraft skills.

SKIING EQUIPMENT NEEDED: Mountain touring gear, or general touring gear if skis are metal-edged, and boots suitable for crossing hill terrain on foot.

OTHER EQUIPMENT NEEDED: Full mountain equipment.

SNOW COVER: Excellent. Enjoys a long season.

APPROACH ROADS: B970 to Feshiebridge, and then minor road up E side of Glen Feshie. Roadside parking just above Achlean.

A tour to a mountain of Munro status across terrain reserved for cross-country ski touring. It includes three really enjoyable descents.

From Achlean a broad and well defined path leads E up the N bank of the Allt Fhearnagan to the Moine Mhor. It ascends steadily, but is a quick and ready means to the snowfields of the plateau. From the path there are good views of the descent route used in return and snow cover and possibilities can be studied. The path does not go to the summit of Carn Ban Mor, but it is worth ascending this rounded hill in order to get maximum enjoyment from the run down the far side. The summit lies N of the path and is approached across easy slopes. It is not immediately obvious, but is marked by a small circular shelter and cairn.

From Carn Ban Mor the route descends to the frozen Loch nan Cnapan, 2.5kms to the SE, initially following the course of the Allt Sgairnich. This is a burn which holds the snow beautifully, and frequently ribbons of skiable snow are preserved here to the end of

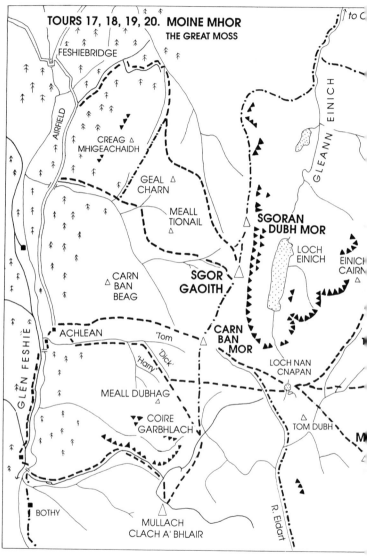

TOURS 17, 18, 19, 20. MOINE MHOR
THE GREAT MOSS

FESHIEBRIDGE

to C

AIRFIELD

GLEANN EINICH

CREAG △
MHIGEACHAIDH

GEAL △
CHARN

MEALL
TIONAIL
△

SGORAN
DUBH MOR △

LOCH
EINICH

EINICH
CAIRN
△

CARN △
BAN
BEAG

SGOR △
GAOITH

ACHLEAN

'Tom'
'Dick'
'Harry'

CARN △
BAN
MOR

LOCH NAN
CNAPAN

GLEN FESHIE

MEALL DUBHAG
△

COIRE
GARBHLACH

△
TOM DUBH

M

R. Eidart

BOTHY

MULLACH △
CLACH A' BHLAIR

spring. The descent is a relaxing romp over an open, unrestricting easy-angled snow field with the security of a long run out ahead. It should be noted that the cliffs at the head of Gleann Einich lie to the NE.

The Allt Sgairnich turns S to contribute to the River Eidart. It is an interesting thought that from the summit of Carn Ban Mor one can ski a 25km descent to the start point by following the Allt Sgairnich, and rivers Eidart and Feshie. Technical skills are less important for the completion of this journey than the ability to cover the distance.

However, the route to Monadh Mor leaves the burn to descend easily to Loch nan Cnapan. Although frozen and possibly snow-covered the lochan can be discerned by its lack of slope, and is one of the navigational reference points for use in mist on the Great Moss.

Ski SE from the lochan, to skirt the NE flank of Tom Dubh, and gain the snow-holding tributary of the Allt Luineag. Continue up a steepening, but short ascent to the broad N ridge and flat boulder-strewn summit of Monadh Mor. The crest of the ridge is often blown clear of snow.

Return to Loch nan Cnapan via the route of ascent. Be wary of skiing too far to the SW, otherwise some ascent from the Allt Luineag will be necessary. It is an uncomplicated, traversing descent, the main concentration point being how to get the most enjoyment from it. Using the most westerly discernible point of the lochan as a reference point ski due W over gently rising slopes for 3kms to the col between Carn Ban Mor and Meall Dubhag. The descent can be made down one of the three tributaries which join to create the Allt Fhearnagan. These three are known as "Tom", "Dick" and "Harry". Tom is the most northerly burn of the three, Dick the middle burn, and Harry, itself made of three tributaries, occupies Coire Gorm. Of the three Dick is the most popular ski run. Tom and Harry are narrower and steeper. Banks of snow build up to allow wide traverses across the burn known as Dick. From the col there is 0.5km easy skiing across a kindly angled snow field, which then channels the skier into the gully proper. It is a magic descent.

At the confluence of Dick with Tom the slope eases and often this is the limit of snow cover. If this is the case, traverse the heather on the N bank of the Allt Fhearnagan to gain the good track leading down to Achlean. If snow cover extends into the glen itself, follow the burn on easy slopes until reaching the open stance of trees. The slopes steepen here, and the burn falls over a waterfall, attractive in itself and bridged at the bottom. However, just before the steep fall, gain the track heading NW and return on this to the start point.

18. BRAERIACH AND CAIRN TOUL

OS SHEET: 36   START POINT: End of public road, GR 852976

TOTAL DISTANCE: 31.5kms   ASCENT: 1402m   TIME: 10 hours 15 minutes

TERRAIN: Good track leading to extensive tundra plateau. Snow-filled burns. Ideal Nordic touring terrain.

SKIING ABILITIES REQUIRED: Ability to cover enormous distances on skis. Good climbing, traverse and descent techniques.

OTHER ABILITIES REQUIRED: Strength and fitness to cover the distance. Excellent winter navigation and hillcraft skills.

SKIING EQUIPMENT NEEDED: Mountain touring gear.

OTHER EQUIPMENT NEEDED: Full mountain equipment.

SNOW COVER: Excellent. Enjoys a long season.

APPROACH ROADS: B970 to Feshiebridge, and then minor road up E side of Glen Feshie. Roadside parking just above Achlean.

A long tour crossing the expanse of the Moine Mhor to reach the third and fourth highest mountains in Great Britain. Remarkably for the great distance involved skiable snow can be expected along much of the route in all but the poorest of snow-bearing winters, and snow cover can still be very good at the end of an average season. Indeed spring is the best time to ski this tour, as that is when daylight is sufficient and the winter's snow has accumulated. If visibility is poor, there is little point in undertaking the excursion. Only the problems are then superlative. Save this one for a brilliant day, when you can see for miles and gallop the descents with glee.

The length of the tour and the time/energy available may determine a shortening of the route. If it comes to a choice between the two mountains the following might be noted. Braeriach is the higher of the two, although only by 5m! Cairn Toul is slightly nearer in distance travelled to Achlean, the round trip being 2.5kms shorter than to ski to Braeriach and back. Braeriach offers easier slopes: Cairn Toul more exciting ones. The summit of Braeriach nudges vertical cliffs, and the route to it skirts the cliffs above An Garbh Choire. Although there are awesome cliffs immediately N of Cairn Toul navigational activities are more unnerving in the approach to Braeriach. Each mountain has its own merits with regard to the potential views one might be fortunate enough to see from the summit cairns.

One compromise for the happy band who do not need to climb a Munro to justify the value of a tour is to ski to Braeriach's SW Top, the rounded summit height 1265m, GR 939983. There are worthwhile views of the terrific precipices of An Garbh Choire from here, and a top-class descent back to Loch nan Cnapan.

From Achlean follow the route to Loch nan Cnapan in the middle of the Great Moss, as described in Tour 17, the ascent of Monadh Mor. From the lochan ski E for 1.5kms, across both tributaries of the Allt Luineag, to gain the SW ridge of Sgor an Lochain Uaine, the Angel's Peak. The route ascends part way up this ridge before crossing onto the slopes above the Allt Clais an t-Sabhail, and finally approaches the summit of Cairn Toul up the steep SW flank. This slope is affected by the sun, and hence may be icy. The summit itself may be stripped clear, revealing unskiable boulders.

Despite the close proximity of cliffs there is a feeling of space on this fine peak. On a clear day views of the Cairngorm Mountains are extensive, and much of the route to Braeriach and from Carn Ban Mor is in evidence.

Descend the broad SW flank for 150m and traverse below the Angel's Peak. The route crosses the SW ridge of the Angel's Peak, descends to the col, and then ascends the easy ridge to the rounded summit of Braeriach's SW Top. Keep well back from the cliffs which drop to An Garbh Choire. They are likely to be carrying huge cornices. From the small cairn at this summit the slopes leading across the plateau to the summit of Braeriach come as a respite. A long and gentle descent leads to a kind ascent. Be wary again of cornicing on the terrific cliffs immediately S and E of the summit. In mist the summit cairn can easily be confused with other cairns hereabouts.

From Braeriach's summit the view over Strathspey, the hotels in Aviemore, the A9 and vegetated land contrast sharply to the harshness of this life-resistant plateau. Towards Cairn Toul perfect corries pander to geography textbook standards.

Return to Braeriach's SW Top and then turn SSW to reach the upper course of the Allt Luineag. This is an excellent snow-holding area, and the run down quite superb. Leave the course of the burn at about a height of 920m to cross ever-decreasing gradients to return to Loch nan Cnapan. It is worth noting that if you are shy of reascending the 40m height required to regain Braeriach's SW Top, and you traverse its NW flank, descending the ridge above the Allt Luineag is not as good a run as that to the burn and along its course. It would be a shame to miss one of the highlights of the tour for just 4 minutes-worth of easy ascent.

From Loch nan Cnapan the route back to Achlean is as for that described in Tour 17, the ascent of Monadh Mor, with the descent of the Allt Fhearnagan a fitting end to a great ski tour.

19. MULLACH CLACH A' BHLAIR .

OS SHEETS: 35, 43   START POINT: End of public road, GR 852976
TOTAL DISTANCE: 17.5kms   ASCENT: 730m   TIME: 5 hours 35 minutes

TERRAIN: Broad road and track leading to gentle undulating plateau. Ascent steep in places. Descent down snow-filled burn.

SKIING ABILITIES REQUIRED: Ability to ascend steep track. Good basic skills of descent.

OTHER ABILITIES REQUIRED: Excellent winter navigation and hillcraft skills. General fitness.

SKIING EQUIPMENT NEEDED: General touring gear - steel edges if icy.

OTHER EQUIPMENT NEEDED: Full mountain equipment.

SNOW COVER: Excellent on the plateau itself, with some skiing often possible as early as November and as late as May. The descent burns defy their westerly aspect and hold snow well to the confluence at 575m, often skiable to this point at Easter. Lower along the road, only skiable when snow is lying below 350m. Snow cover for much of the route can be checked from the A9 at Kingussie.

APPROACH ROADS: B970 to Feshiebridge, and then minor road up E side of Glen Feshie. Roadside parking just above Achlean.

A circular tour linking terrain, approaches and routes of skiing significance which may be skied as a full tour, as described below, or incorporated into other tours.

The existence of good approaches and gentle slopes on the plateau give a sense of ease and relaxation about this tour. However complacency is not appropriate, since all the problems of the plateau, in particular the problems of navigating in mist may well arise. The route goes precariously close to the cliffs of Coire Garbhlach, and with precious little to navigate by in poor visibility it takes complete mastery of navigational skills on skis to find the safe descent.

The tour can be skied in a clockwise direction. This gives the advantage of getting the ascent over and done with first, and of reaching the snow on the plateau quickly when there is none in the glen. However, the best ski runs are to be had if the route is skied

anticlockwise, the views in all sections of the tour are more spectacular, it is less likely that deer will be disturbed, and the descent leads
directly to the start point.

If snow cover is restricted to the High Plateau then ascending the
Allt Fhearnagan path and approaching the summit across the Moine
Mhor, to return as for the main route gives the maximum amount of
time on skis. The skiing for this alternative is no more difficult than
for the main tour.

Skirt around the farm and head S on paths, to the bridge over the
River Feshie 1km beyond the farm. Cross the bridge and ski along the
private road on the W bank of the river. The road is barred to public
traffic by a locked gate at Tolvah, and is not cleared, although
vehicles may have passed along it to Carnachuin. It gives easy skiing
on a tarmac base over gently undulating slopes. Glen Feshie is
beautiful here, a choice place to ski on a fine day - or in moonlight too
for that matter.

Shortly after Carnachuin a steep and tricky track on the left leads
down to a bridge. Cross the bridge to gain the track leading E up the
hillside just N of the Allt Coire Chaoil.

Slightly off route, but well worth noting is Ruigh-aiteachain bothy,
which lies 1km SSE of the bridge. This bothy is maintained by the
Mountain Bothies Association. It is in good condition, and provides
excellent overnight shelter. It is a convenient base for skiing expeditions on the Great Moss. When there is snow cover in the glen an
easy ski to the bothy for lunch, and then back to either Achlean or
Tolvah would make a super family ski outing. The bothy is set back
from the track, just after a small stance of trees.

It is a long steep haul up the track, which winds around the hillside
to a col on the ridge marking the margin of Coire Garbhlach. A
window view at the col gives a fine insight into the deep cut, and
emphasises the danger that complacency on the gentle plateau could
lead to. Coire Garbhlach is one of the few W-facing corries in
Scotland.

Upon reaching the plateau the track divides. Go S for 1km from this
point, and thus reach easily the bald summit of Mullach Clach a'
Bhlair. The track does not lead to the summit, but skirts its N flank.
It is no longer of significance to this tour, but it is worth noting that
drifted snow collects on the track, and can give good skiing when the
surrounding moor has been stripped of snow. Early skiing on the

track is sometimes possible before the rest of the moor comes into condition.

From the summit ski NE on easy slopes down a broad snow field to the rounded lump at GR 891944, height 953m. Continue N for 1.5kms to the col between Carn Ban Mor and Meall Dubhag - the start of the descent run down the Allt Fhearnagan - see Tour 17. In good conditions the section from Mullach Clach a' Bhlair across the plateau is a straightforward romp, with spectacular views of Sgor Gaoith and Sgoran Dubh Mor to the N, across the plateau towards Braeriach to the E, and down Coire Garbhlach to the W. In poor conditions it is a hazardous journey, where precise route finding is imperative. Do not rely on finding the track or the precise course of the burns. These are likely to be buried and not apparent.

20. SGOR GAOITH

OS SHEET: 36   START POINT: Entrance to forest, GR 852012

TOTAL DISTANCE: 17.5kms   ASCENT: 840m   TIME: 5 hours 45 minutes

TERRAIN: Mixed terrain of open moorland, summit ridge, snow-filled burns and forest road. Ascent steep in places. Ridge prone to icing.

SKIING ABILITIES REQUIRED: Ability to ascend steep and icy slopes. Descent requires reliable traverse and snowplough at least.

OTHER ABILITIES REQUIRED: Excellent winter navigation and hillcraft skills and general fitness.

SKIING EQUIPMENT NEEDED: Mountain touring gear.

OTHER EQUIPMENT NEEDED: Full mountain equipment.

SNOW COVER: Excellent in burns and corries. Ridge may be blown clear. Lower moor and forest not reliable, although forest shade preserves snow cover after thaw elsewhere. In upper sections snow cover still suitable in late season. Descent burn can be seen from A9 between Kingussie and Aviemore.

APPROACH ROADS: B970 to Feshiebridge, then minor road up E side of Glen Feshie. Roadside parking at start point.

An excellent tour through varied terrain to a lofty viewpoint. It involves all types of skiing from easy forest tracks to taxing mountain slopes. The downhill run from the summit and along the Allt a Mharcaidh is notably good.

Shortly before the minor Glen Feshie road bridges the Allt Ruadh a broad track delves E into the forest. Follow this for 0.5km to the meeting of paths at the boundary of the Cairngorm Nature Reserve. Continue E through woods on a wide path which climbs steadily up the steep N bank of the river. Upon reaching the open moor turn SE and ski 0.5kms to the confluence of streams at GR 875007. The route continues below Meall Tionail in a rising traverse S to meet the Allt a' Chrom-alltain. (Path this far if snow cover is lacking.)

The various branches of the Allt a' Chrom-alltain all hold the snow beautifully, and any of them can be chosen to access the summit. The skier should assess the best course on arrival, taking account in particular the increasing steepness of the slope towards the summit. Certainly detouring traverses ease the gradient, but even in icy conditions the direct line is possible using skins and good technique.

The last few hundred yards to the summit rise only gently, but they tempt a misleading introduction to the summit of this mountain, which is known for the plunging cliffs falling away immediately beyond slabs on the E side to the inky Loch Einich below. The edge may be corniced. It is an interesting summit, offering unusual views of the Cairngorm Mountains. Sightings of that most endearing little bird, the snow bunting, have been recorded here.

It is reasonable upon leaving Sgor Gaoith to continue to Sgoran Dubh Mor, the slightly lower Munro Top lying just over 1km N along the ridge. This adds only 20 minutes of easy skiing and includes a lively running descent back to the broad open col to regain the main route. However for those not attracted by any more ascent, head N and descend easily to just before the col between Sgor Gaoith and Sgoran Dubh Mor, and then turn NW down a steep, but traversable, bank to the flat ground and easy run out at the watershed separating the Allt a' Chrom-alltain and the Allt a Mharcaidh. Maintaining as much velocity as you dare on the steep descent, speed over this field aiming NW for the source of the Allt a Mharcaidh.

This is an excellent snow holding burn, and often late in season a ribbon of snow extends along its course well after snow melt on the surrounding moor. It is a superb run, well suited to cross-country downhill techniques. Initially there is space to play with, but even with narrowing lower down there is plenty of room to manoeuvre. The quality of this run was known as early as 1913. George Sang described the burn as "the run of the day" in a report in the *Scottish Ski Club Journal* describing a ski traverse of the Great Moss from Glen Geusachan on 22 March that year.

After 2kms the valley opens up and the snow cover can be less complete. If snow cover has expired a path traverses the moor below Geal-charn and then down the broad ridge to enter the woods at GR 884039. If there is snow continue NW over easy slopes to enter the woods at the same corner.

Descend through trees to the Allt a Mharcaidh. 0.5km downstream find a footbridge just before a gate in the tall deer fence. On the other side of the fence there is a large turning area on a broad forest road. Ski easily down the road, and turning left at a junction after 1km return to meet the public road at the Glen Feshie Airstrip. If transport has not been arranged return to the start point 2kms S along the road.

An interesting route of return traverses around Geal-charn to ascend the Allt nan Cuileach to the col between Creag Mhigeachaidh and Geal-charn, continuing SSW to rejoin the outward route at GR 870010. This alternative gives straightforward skiing on the moor itself, but descending the path down the river bank is quite tricky, being steep, restricted, often icy and uncomfortably near the drop down to the river. This alternative route may offer snow when the lower reaches have none and the snow cover can be checked on the outward journey. It is a more direct route back for those having to return to the start point and avoids the tricky descent through the woods along the Allt a Mharcaidh. A deer fence along the moor section aids navigation. Indeed on days when touring the High Tops is out of the question quite a pleasant circular tour can be enjoyed by linking a crossing of the col with sheltered skiing along the same forest roads which the main route uses.

21. INSHRIACH FOREST

OS SHEET: 35 or 36 START POINT: End of forest road at GR 853044

TOTAL DISTANCE: 8.5kms   ASCENT: 130m   TIME: 2 hours 20 minutes

TERRAIN: Broad forest roads. Mostly easy gradients, but also some steep sections.

SKIING ABILITIES REQUIRED: Majority of tour very easy and suitable for beginners. One steep hill with bends requires good snowplough or stickbrake technique.

OTHER ABILITIES REQUIRED: Elementary map reading skills.

SKIING EQUIPMENT NEEDED: Light touring gear.

OTHER EQUIPMENT NEEDED: Lightweight equipment.

SNOW COVER: The land lies between 250m and 300m above sea level. Snow cover is unpredictable and snow does not linger except in a prolonged cold spell. However the forest roads constitute a good base and minimum snow cover is required to ski them. This is a peak season tour.

APPROACH ROADS: B970 to Feshiebridge, then minor road leading to Achlean. Parking is at the road side, immediately S of the junction with the B970.

This is a tour for those who like to ski on broad, easy tracks, through forest. Fortunately there are some sections of ascent and descent, and bends and twists of the track to enliven an otherwise unchallenging and monotonous jaunt through plantations of conifers.

Leave the minor Achlean road and follow the broad and gently rising forest track leading NE through the trees. After 0.5km turn sharp left at a junction and keep on the road track for a further 1km until a crossroads is reached. There are tempting glimpses of the Monadhliath Mountains to the W and Geal-charn and surrounding rounded ridges of the Cairngorm foothills to the S. Off-shoots from the main track intrigue curiosity.

At the crossroads a left turn would quickly take you down to the B970 road, so turn right instead, and bury yourself deeper into the forest. Ignore a track leading away to the right and continue to a fork.

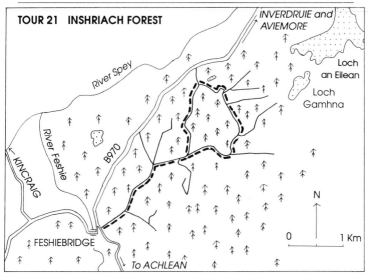

This is the moment of choice. The next section of the route is a circle which can be skied in either direction. An anticlockwise direction tackles the steepest slope as a descent. The slope is fast and fun as it winds downhill. However, it would daunt the less able, who may prefer to ascend it. The clockwise choice gives the steepest section in ascent, whilst the descent occurs over a longer and more gentle gradient. Take the right fork for anticlockwise, the left fork for clockwise direction. The anticlockwise direction is described here.

From the fork continue along the broad track until the road swings round to the left. Here a track leads straight ahead, but this heads out of the forest and over moorland. It can be followed to Loch an Eilean and linked with the Glen More trails. The main tour, however, keeps in the trees, and climbs stiffly. Keep left at the next junction and continue ascending until a new track, not marked on some OS maps is reached. This is the top of the climb. Go straight on, and keep left at the next junction. The road immediately dives left. Soon the slope eases and there is a run out to the next junction. A frozen lochan hides away in the woods to the right.

At the junction turn left and begin the climb back. The right fork leads to the B970. The track undulates for 1.5kms, but there is no doubt that overall the slope is uphill. Eventually the loop is completed and the outward route is regained. Return to the start point along your own tracks.

THE MONADHLIATH - THE GREY MOORS

The vast area of undulating moorland NW of the River Spey, E of Loch Ness and S of the A9 between Carrbridge and Tomatin contains some of the best Nordic touring terrain in Scotland. Here are many square kilometres of easy slopes and shallow burns, mostly above 600m. It is the Monadh Liath that occupies much of this area - the Grey Moors. They are not attractive to walkers, who have described them as drab, dreary and depressing, but to the skier they give good sport. They offer extensive views, and in the SE section there are spectacular crags and corries.

The area is not as popular as the neighbouring Cairngorms. However it is sometimes possible to ski in the Monadhliath when conditions in these mightier mountains are not suitable. Indeed early in the season the grass, heather and moss on the Monadhliath may give a skiable base when the stony tundra of Cairn Gorm is blown clear. Unfortunately they do not preserve the snow as well as the Cairngorms, and have a shorter season.

The most popular part is that closest to Strathspey above Newtonmore, Kingussie and Aviemore. Certainly this is the highest part, with four mountains of Munro status. It is also the most sculptured and shaped by glacial action with craggy corries and scooped out glens. But primarily it is the most accessible part with the arterial A9 along its margin and a series of Land-Rover tracks leading N from the Strathspey settlements. The more northerly areas are not well penetrated by roads.

There are many traverses along the watersheds and shallow burns. Some can be completed in a day, others require longer retreats. The more lengthy routes include skiing from Aviemore to Fort Augustus, Slochd to Newtonmore, Geal Charn (GR 561988) to Geal-charn Mor (GR 837123), or Tomatin to Loch Mhor. Route choice will depend very much on wind direction on the day, but also that of the preceding weeks for it is the wind that is responsible for the distribution of the snow here and the resulting snow cover.

All four Munros can be approached via relatively easy slopes and linked together as one high level traverse. However it is usual to ski Geal Charn on a separate outing simply because of the distance involved and transport problems returning to the start point.

22. THE MONADHLIATH MUNROS

OS SHEET: 35   START POINT: End of public road, GR 692997

TOTAL DISTANCE: 28kms ASCENT: 1060m TIME: 8 hours 45 mins

TERRAIN: Open moorland, mostly easy slopes.

SKIING ABILITIES REQUIRED: Basic skills of ascent, traverse and descent. Ability to cover long distances.

OTHER ABILITIES REQUIRED: Excellent navigation and hillcraft skills.

SKIING EQUIPMENT NEEDED: General touring gear - steel edges if icy.

OTHER EQUIPMENT NEEDED: Full mountain equipment.

SNOW COVER: Good on higher slopes, not reliable in the glen. Ideal base requiring little cover. Snow usually redistributed by the wind.

APPROACH ROADS: From Newtonmore main street take the minor road leading NW into Glen Banchor. Parking at end of public road.

This is a long tour on generally easy terrain. Navigation is simplified in the middle section by following a line of fence posts between Carn Ban (also known as Carn Mairg) and Carn Sgulain. Some of the route can be seen from the A9 and thus the extent of the snow cover anticipated. It links three Munro Summits and includes a 14km stretch above the 800m contour line. There are many opportunities to explore terrain beyond the route, or to shorten it. The wind direction on the day will influence which way round the circuit is skied but note the run down from A' Chailleach to the start point is very good. If the snow line is high it may be preferable to follow the shorter route (see Alternative 1) and utilise the good Land-Rover track on the E bank of the Allt Fionndrigh to walk to the snow. This route could also be used when the burns are swollen with snow melt, as the Allt

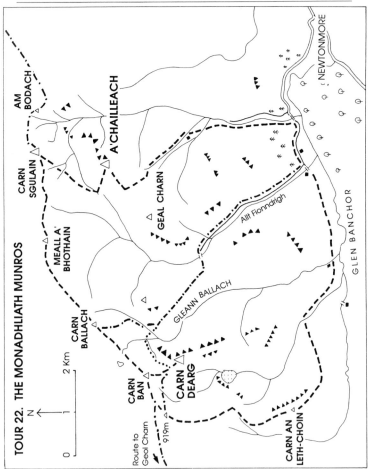

TOUR 22. THE MONADHLIATH MUNROS

Fionndrigh is bridged at GR 659019 (footbridge), but it may not be easy to cross the Allt Ballach if in spate on the route up Glen Banchor.

The route is described in a clockwise direction as this gives better running, it saves the best descent for the end of the day, and makes most use of the prevailing westerlies. From the start point go W up Glen Banchor. There is a Land-Rover track as far as Gleann Ballach. From there easy skiing up the open glen leads past Dalballoch to the Allt an Lochain Duibh, which should be followed briefly N and then crossed to reach the slopes flanking the N of Sron na Creige. Thus the SW ridge of Carn an Leth-choin can easily be ascended. Continue N to the long rise leading to the line of fence posts and the domed summit, height 919m. The fence posts can be followed E along the route to Carn Sgulain, but if an ascent of Carn Dearg is to be included ski due E to the col N of Carn Dearg's summit and then approach this Munro from that point. Note the crags immediately E of this ascent, where cornices build up. Return to the col and ascend Carn Ban. Follow the line of fence posts along the watershed via Carn Ballach and Meall a' Bhothain to Carn Sgulain. These are very easy enjoyable kilometres. The large summit cairn of A' Chailleach is the next destination. It has been in evidence along the route (visibility permitting) and appears easily attainable. However between Carn Sgulain and A' Chailleach the Allt Cuil na Caillich has incised a trough, the S bank of which is surprisingly steep, and presents an obstacle. It is easier to ski SW from Carn Sgulain to the headwaters of the culprit burn and then ascend E to A' Chailleach's summit.

A' Chailleach belies the description of dreariness and depression given by some visitors to the Monadhliath. It sports a plunging coire of crags on its E flank, which is impressive when viewed from Am Bodach. There is also good ski running from the summit. It is quite an easy Munro to ski and can be quickly bagged from the start point (approximate ascent time 2 hours 30 minutes). Since it can be seen from the A9 and the snow cover confirmed it is a popular destination for the Speyside based skier.

To return to the start point ski SW for 0.5km from the summit and then turn SE down broad and gentle slopes to reach the burns leading past a wooden hut known as the "Red Bothy". This is a good run. Ski S from the bothy to just W of the bridge at the start point. If snow cover does not permit skiing at lower levels cross the Allt a' Chaorainn (aim for a high crossing if burns are in spate) and return via the track on the E bank.

Alternatives

1. Ascent of Carn Dearg from Gleann Ballach

Follow the broad track heading up the E side of the Allt Fionndrigh
and cross this at the footbridge GR 659019. Ascend W and pass into
Gleann Ballach. Continue up the E side of the glen dominated by
Carn Dearg's classy E face. There is a direct route from the head of the
glen trending SW to the col between Carn Dearg and Carn Ban. This
is steep and requires skins, confidence and ability in addition to good
judgement of the safeness of the snow. It is an exciting descent for
those with the relevant qualifications. A safer and much easier route
ascends to the snow bowl NW of Meall na Ceardaich. The line of fence
posts is gained and Carn Dearg approached from Carn Ban.

2. E of Carn Sgulain

E of Carn Sgulain lies some eminently skiable terrain and a choice of
routes back to Strathspey along a series of excellent tracks. It is quite
feasible given time and energy to ski to Aviemore. The fence posts

Synchronized telemarking in the Monadhliath Hills. Looking S to A' Chailleach and Geal Charn from Meall a' Bhothain

continue to Am Bodach, but then turn N.

The track leading N from Kingussie merits special note as it rises to a height of 760m above sea level and can be used as a launch pad for an ascent of Carn an Fhreiceadain. It was marked on Roy's map of 1755 as a route between Kingussie and Tomatin. Carn an Fhreiceadain was in fact skied by 3 skisters in February 1906, one of the first ski tours for pleasure recorded in this country. A member of the party, Allan Arthur, describes the trip in glowing terms in Volume 10 (1906-9) of the *SMC Journal*. Conditions that day were perfect and the sun blazing hot, yet he boasts the snow was "as keen and dry as any I ever skied on in Switzerland". Skiing in those days was so unusual that when the skisters arrived back in Kingussie a crowd of about 200 lined the road to witness their return.

If approaching from Kingussie a car can be driven as far as the golf course, but the road beyond to Pitmain Lodge is private. A track branches W from the main track and descends to an unlocked bothy in good condition at the confluence GR 723052. The hut at the point where the track crosses the Allt Mor GR 734050 is on the other hand

High level touring in the Monadhliath Hills. Looking SSW from Carn Ballach to Carn Dearg

a ruin. The tributaries joining the Allt Mor from the N hold the snow and give a good descent route back to the track.

3. W of Carn Ban

The high area W of the route offers further good Nordic touring terrain. It is possible to ski to Geal Charn from Carn Ban on a route of approximately 9kms length which does not drop below 800m nor rise above 900m. The escape routes back to Strathspey are not as copious, easy or straightforward as those from routes further E. Crossing the Markie Burn in Glen Markie to gain the track on the E bank can be a problem.

23. LOCHNAGAR AND THE WHITE MOUNTH

OS SHEETS: 43 and 44   START POINT: Invercauld Bridge, GR 186910
TOTAL DISTANCE: 24kms   ASCENT: 1050m   TIME: 7 hours 45 minutes

TERRAIN: Forest track through natural pine forest leading to heather moorland and extensive high level tundra plateau.

SKIING ABILITIES REQUIRED: Slopes mostly easy. Basic skills of ascent, traverse and descent. Ability to cope with difficult snow and cover the distance.

OTHER ABILITIES REQUIRED: Excellent winter navigation skills.

SKIING EQUIPMENT NEEDED: General touring gear - steel edges if icy.

OTHER EQUIPMENT NEEDED: Full mountain equipment.

SNOW COVER: Excellent on the plateau - enjoys a long season. Snow holds in ribbons along the N-facing burns in late season. Track unreliable. Requires snow at 300m to ski whole route.

APPROACH ROADS: A93 Braemar to Ballater. Roadside parking.

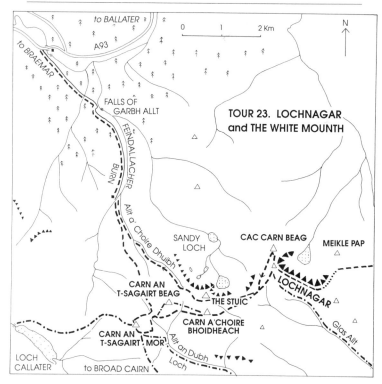

Note: This route passes through the Balmoral Royal Estate where access is different from elsewhere in Scotland since the security of those staying at Balmoral is a consideration. Anyone considering approaching via the Ballochbuie Forest as described here, should first contact the Resident Factor, Balmoral Estate, Ballater (Estate Office: Telephone 033 84 334).

This tour leads through a rich variety of unique landscapes to one of Scotland's finest mountains. The spectacular cliffs of Lochnagar are a beautiful sight to travellers on Royal Deeside and are famous for their winter climbing routes. However it is the vast plateau extending S and W of Lochnagar that is of interest to skiers. Many kilometres of broad snow slopes undulate above the 900m contour line, acknowledging a wealth of Munro Summits and tempting the skier to long traverses across easy terrain. If circumstances permit this tour can be just one part of a larger excursion. However it is a tour of quality in its own right, traversing three Munro Summits, with superb views, excellent running and an approach of unrivalled beauty through the natural pine forest of Ballochbuie. In poor visibility navigation on the plateau must be precise yet there are limited reference points. There is no shelter on the plateau from the winds which batter the expanse. Save this one for a good day.

Leave the A93 immediately W of where the road crosses the River Dee at Invercauld and enter the forest on a good track leading SE past the grand old bridge over the Dee. This carried the military road before the new bridge made it redundant. Looking from the main road its humped back figures a romantic foreground to the backdrop of the forest and mountains above - a view incidentally of the route ahead.

Ascend good tracks through the forest maintaining a SE direction at track junctions until the route sweeps SW at the Falls of Garbh Allt. Just beyond this bend turn left to continue along the excellent forest track W of the Feindallacher Burn. Ballochbuie Forest is a unique and beautiful forest. It is reputed to be the oldest of the highland forests, said never to have been felled. It was saved from exploitation and destruction by Queen Victoria's purchase of Balmoral. She would not permit the felling of a forest she referred to as the "bonniest plaid in Scotland". Today it exists very much in its natural form, although the red deer prevent re-growth outwith areas protected by deer fencing. There are trees 200 years old - magnificent spreading gnarled Scots pines. The falls of Garbh Allt are just off the route and the bridge above them is well worth making a short detour to. The tracks are broad and well graded, although the gradient stutters, giving some short steep sections, exciting in descent. To ski them is magical. But if snow is not lingering they give a fast walking route to skiing on higher ground.

From the end of the track at a turning point and small shelter cross the Feindallacher Burn. Carn an t-Sagairt Beag and Carn an t-Sagairt Mor (often called Carn Taggart) lie immediately ahead, and the route ascends to the col between them. In late season snow holds in ribbons along the E flanks of the broad heathery ridge W of the Allt a' Choire Dhuibh and presents a skiable corridor of ascent. If snow cover is not complete it is worth identifying those ribbons or patches which might be useful on the descent route. From the col follow the line of fence posts up steep but broad slopes, past the wing of an aircraft to the elongated flat summit of Carn an t-Sagairt Mor. This is stony and may be blown clear. There are tremendous views in all directions, but it is the enormity of the ski touring potential on the White Mounth that is most exciting. The route ahead to the dome of Carn a' Choire Bhoidheach is apparent in good visibility and the best line to it can be chosen. It is possible to ski over Carn an t-Sagairt Beag or to contour around its S flanks. The slopes steepen briefly in places, but are always broad enough to allow easy angled traverses. Note that cornicing does occur on the tributaries of the Allt an Dubh-loch. There are imposing cliffs to the N at The Stuic, which are passed on the return route.

From the summit of Carn a' Choire Bhoidheach a long and gradual descent leads over the vast snow field at the head of Coire Boidheach to a short steep ascent and the final summit plateau of Lochnagar. This is superb skiing in good visibility, with exciting views back over the cliffs of The Stuic to the imposing Cairngorm Massif. In poor visibility good compass and map work are required to find the safe corridor between sudden plunging cliff-lines.

The high point of Lochnagar, Cac Carn Beag, is an elevated pedestal - a granite tor - above the summit plateau, lying just N of the famous cliffs. The mountain was once called the White Mounth, but this name now refers to the plateau area to the S and W, which allows the skier such an easy approach. On a clear day there is a panorama of many mountains and the useful indicator provided suggests one might see as far as Ben Nevis to the W, Bell Rock Lighthouse in the North Sea or to the Cheviot in the S. The cliffs of the mountain's NE corrie plunge dizzily down and are heavily corniced, so it is with great care and due regard that their pinnacles and buttresses might be glimpsed.

Return S to the headwaters of the Glas Allt and keeping N of the outward route ski W above steep slopes and cliffs to The Stuic. This is a rocky platform and may well be blown clear and unskiable. It can be bypassed, but is worth visiting in clear visibility for the elevated view across Royal Deeside.

Descend broad slopes W to the Allt a' Choire Dhuibh, which is then followed to the confluence with the Feindallacher Burn. Retrace the outward route through the Ballochbuie Forest sanctuary enjoying views through the open woods to Ben Avon and Beinn a' Bhuird.

Alternatives

1. From Loch Muick

The route to the summit of Lochnagar from the car park at Spittal of Glenmuick is the shortest and most popular route for walkers. The usual walkers' route ascends to the col S of Meikle Pap and then climbs very steeply the exposed ridge at the end of the cliff-lined corrie. This allows exceptional views of the cliffs, but for skiers requires advanced climbing techniques on skins and good judgement. Ice axe and crampons may be needed. It is not a descent route for skiers. An easier route following more gentle slopes leaves the Land-Rover track and crosses the Monelpie Moss to the course of the Glas Allt, which is then ascended to the White Mounth. The Glas Allt holds snow well, although the lower section of this route may be snow-free. If so a good path leads steeply past the waterfalls above Glas-allt-Shiel to link with the Land-Rover track along the N of Loch Muick.

From Carn an t-Sagairt Mor it is possible to descend gradually to Loch Muick along the Allt an Dubh-loch past the Dubh Loch. However this requires good snow cover at low levels or a long walk.

2. From Glen Callater

It is possible to reach the White Mounth from the A93 S of Braemar via Glen Callater. This route utilises the Tolmount drove road as far as Lochcallater Lodge and then strikes up the slopes N of Loch Callater to approach Carn an t-Sagairt Mor on broad flanks from the W.

3. To Broad Cairn

It is less than 5kms of easy skiing from Carn an t-Sagairt Mor via Cairn Bannoch to Broad Cairn. The stony tundra may be blown clear in places, otherwise this is an excellent high level traverse. From Broad Cairn descents can be made to Spittal of Glenmuick, Glen Clova via Route 31, Glen Doll via Route 30 or 31, or to the A93 via Route 24. The A93 can be reached more directly by traversing the long and easy ridge of Fafernie to Knaps of Fafernie and Tolmount, thus bypassing Cairn Bannoch.

24. GLEN SHEE TO BROAD CAIRN

OS SHEETS: 43 and 44   START POINT: Glenshee Ski-lift Car Park, GR 141779

TOTAL DISTANCE: 26kms   ASCENT: 1070m (760m on outward journey)

TIME: 8 hours 20 minutes (not using ski lifts)

TERRAIN: Steep slopes leading to a wide open plateau. Once on plateau easy slopes between a series of broad summits.

SKIING ABILITIES REQUIRED: Ability to climb, traverse and descend steep slopes, negotiate ice and mixed rock and ice, and cover long distances.

OTHER ABILITIES REQUIRED: Excellent winter navigation and hillcraft skills and high level of fitness.

SKIING EQUIPMENT NEEDED: Mountain touring gear essential.

OTHER EQUIPMENT NEEDED: Full mountain equipment.

SNOW COVER: Summits may be blown clear. Otherwise excellent. Enjoys a long season.

APPROACH ROADS: A93 Blairgowrie to Braemar. Parking at start point.

A Munro Bagger's delight. This tour links four Munro Summits and takes the skier within easy skiing of several other summits and tops which it is quite feasible to add to the day's collection.

Purists will insist on climbing on foot to Meall Odhar, but for others there is the option to use the uplift facilities of the Glenshee Chairlift Company Limited. This saves 250m climbing - which translates into a saving of time and energy for more enjoyable skiing away from the madding crowd.

From the S end of the car parks go E up a broad track over a rise to the bowl at the foot of the Meall Odhar Tow. Ascend the ridge to the right of the tow. From the top of the Meall Odhar Tow turn SE and pass by the cairn on the top of Meall Odhar itself. The route ascends very steeply the NW shoulder of Glas Maol. With skins this steep gradient can be contemplated on Nordic skis, but many prefer to walk this tricky section. (Either method, care required.) The half

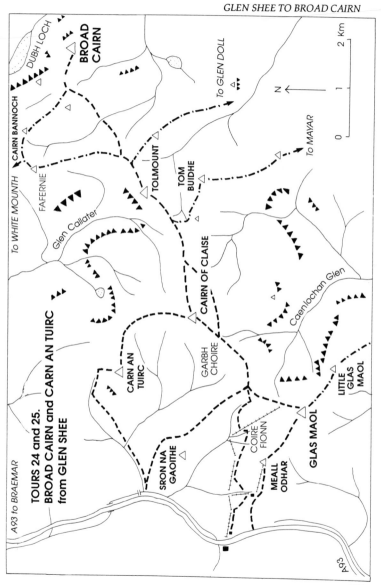

TOURS 24 and 25.
BROAD CAIRN and CARN AN TUIRC
from GLEN SHEE

kilometre leading to the summit of Glas Maol is by contrast almost flat.

From Glas Maol turn NNE and enjoy a kilometre and a half of easy running over a broad snowy expanse before embarking on the gradual ascent to the summit of Cairn of Claise (fence posts). From here the route to Tolmount descends ENE, again over a spacious, gentle gradient for a further pleasant kilometre and a half before ascending easily the broad SW ridge of this, the third Munro Summit of the day.

The route from Tolmount to Broad Cairn passes over a series of cols and the skiers can avoid unnecessary descent and reascent by carefully choosing his route to link these (close scrutiny of map and compass in poor visibility). The boulder-strewn summit of Broad Cairn is approached from the W.

Return via the outward route to Tolmount, and then to save unnecessary ascent traverse around the SE flank of Cairn of Claise and rejoin the outward route on the ridge trending SW from the summit.

From the col, GR 170778, the most direct route back to the car parks descends into the snow bowls of the Allt Coire Fionn, contours around the corries and ridges furnished by the downhill ski development and finally descends the Sunnyside downhill piste. This route is for the skilled. Alternatively the descent of Sron na Gaoithe and the Allt Coire Fionn to join the A93 N of the Cairnwell Pass calls for less skill in both skiing and navigation.

25. CARN AN TUIRC

OS SHEET: 43

START POINT: A93 2kms N of Cairnwell Pass, above bridge across Cairnwell Burn, GR 148800

TOTAL DISTANCE: 11kms   ASCENT: 540m   TIME: 3 hours 40 minutes

TERRAIN: Mountain slopes of all gradients. Base of heather and grass. Rock-strewn summits.

SKIING ABILITIES REQUIRED: For much of the route basic ability to ascend and descend easy slopes. Steeper sections require more experience and skill. Competent traverse and kick turns are possible across the broad flanks, but a cool head is required if icy. In early season or poor snow cover ability to cope with sections of awkward deep heather base.

OTHER ABILITIES REQUIRED: Excellent winter navigation and hillcraft skills.

SKIING EQUIPMENT NEEDED: Mountain touring gear.

OTHER EQUIPMENT NEEDED: Full mountain equipment.

SNOW COVER: Good. Skiable with minimum snow cover. Much of the route can be seen and snow cover checked from A93 at start point.

APPROACH ROADS: A93 Blairgowrie to Braemar. A gap in the crash barrier on the E side allows some parking off the road.

A short mountain circuit offering fine views and exhilarating skiing. There is a good chance of skiable snow cover here before and after it blesses other areas, making this is a possible tour for autumn days when daylight is rationed.

Wind direction on the day will determine which way round the circuit is skied. It is described here going anticlockwise, thus the prevailing south-westerlies will be behind the skier on the high plateau section approaching Cairn of Claise. This direction also gives good ski running on the descent from Carn an Tuirc.

From the start point descend to the Cairnwell Burn and cross this S of its confluence with the Allt a' Gharbh-choire. At the time of writing a rough bridge of metal pipes spans the burn. This allows a dry crossing, but the pipes are usually icy and quite an obstacle. The route ascends towards Sron na Gaoithe from where a broad easy ridge climbs gradually to the Glas Maol Plateau. It is possible to ascend to the ridge from Coire Fionn. However better snow is usually found by heading SE to the N slopes of Sron na Gaoithe which are then ascended on a gently rising traverse E before turning S to ascend the snow bowl which lies E of Sron na Gaoithe. This route also takes one away from the intruding sight of the downhill ski tows in upper Coire Fionn - at least until the crest of the ridge is reached. The ridge is pleasant in ascent or descent, offering extensive views, including a look at the route ahead to Cairn of Claise and Carn an Tuirc.

The ridge joins the plateau at the broad col half-way between Glas Maol and Cairn of Claise. Easy skiing E then NE leads to the large summit cairn of Cairn of Claise. Route finding on this section is assisted in poor visibility by the line of fence posts, indicating the county march between Aberdeenshire and Angus, which run between Glas Maol and Cairn of Claise. From the summit the vast ski-touring potential of this high-level plateau can be appreciated, as some of the best langlauf terrain in the country stretches away to the E of the mountain.

From the summit ski due N down wide and easy slopes to the col before Carn an Tuirc. This N-facing grass-based flank comes quickly into condition and stays that way long. It gives quite wonderful skiing. The col is broad, but take care not to miss it, for both to the W and the E the land falls hurriedly down. From the col turn NW to ascend easily 70m of height in 1km to the summit cairn of Carn an Tuirc. The summit may well be blown clear and skis have to be carried over the inconvenient frost-shattered stone field.

In clear conditions there are extensive views from the summit in all directions including the Cairngorm Massif, the White Mounth and the Glen Shee hills. Much of the route already skied is evident, as are the downhill tows on both sides of the A93.

Ski N from the summit, and after only 400m distance gain the top of a snow gully, leading NW. This is not apparent from the summit dome so take extra care with navigation in poor visibility. Turn NW to descend the gully and its adjacent slopes. This section is steep, requires confidence and a calm mental approach if icy. However, the flank is broad, and the steep section short, with more relaxing terrain immediately ahead. Formerly the Aberdeen Ski Club had a hut and operated a rope tow in this gully, known then as "Turkey Gully". The remains still exist, but may well be covered by the snow.

As the slope eases ski SW over heather-based terrain to meet the Allt a' Gharbh-choire. If snow cover does not extend to the road, a path leads along the N bank of the burn, to the bridge and start point. If snow cover is complete ski easily the slopes above the burn. The S bank gives better skiing.

26. LOCH VROTACHAN

OS SHEET: 43   START POINT: Glenshee Ski-lift Car Park, GR 141779
TOTAL DISTANCE: 6kms   ASCENT: 280m   TIME: 2 hours
TERRAIN: Snow-filled burns - mostly gentle slopes. One short steeper slope.
SKIING ABILITIES REQUIRED: Suit beginner who may walk some sections.
OTHER ABILITIES REQUIRED: Basic winter navigational skills.
SKIING EQUIPMENT NEEDED: General touring gear.
OTHER EQUIPMENT NEEDED: Lightweight equipment. Picnic.
SNOW COVER: Excellent - enjoys long season.
APPROACH ROADS: A93 Blairgowrie to Braemar. Parking at start point.

Man made the Glenshee ski tows for the downhill skier, but God made the area around Loch Vrotachan for cross-country skiers. This area is perfect for "messing about on skis".

Although the tour is short it has much to offer. It is comfortingly near the facilities of the Glenshee downhill development, there are no sections of difficulty and map reading is simplified by following burns. It offers easy terrain for the beginner to practice turns and techniques. For a Cross-country Downhiller telemarking on the Glenshee pistes it presents a short tour when he has used all of his lift ticket or, as happens later in the season, the lifts have closed and there are still plenty of daylight hours left.

Climb the track behind the café and ski past the ski tows, into a

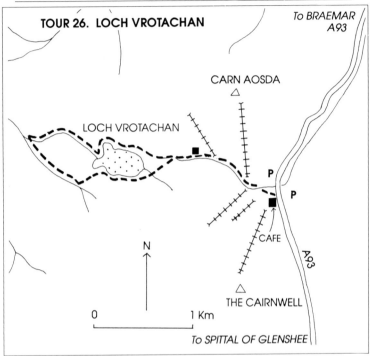

TOUR 26. LOCH VROTACHAN

To BRAEMAR A93

CARN AOSDA

LOCH VROTACHAN

P

P

CAFE

A93

N

THE CAIRNWELL

0   1 Km

To SPITTAL OF GLENSHEE

gully to a small hut. Shortly after passing this hut a col is reached and skiing W leads the skier to a slope above Loch Vrotachan. Skirt the loch on its S bank. A small rise at the end of the loch is flanked on both sides by two burns. The route descends S of the rise along the more southerly of these burns until the confluence with the other burn is reached. Turn NW to follow this burn on easy slopes back to Loch Vrotachan, which is then skirted on the N bank. In prolonged cold conditions the loch freezes and is skiable.

To return to the A93 reverse the outward route. The gully leading down past the hut may prove unnerving to a beginner but the main danger will be collision with downhill skiers.

27. BEINN IUTHARN MHOR

OS SHEET: 43

START POINT: Glenshee Ski-lift and Car Park, GR 141779

TOTAL DISTANCE: 23kms   ASCENT: 815m   TIME: 7 hours

TERRAIN: Mostly moderate undulating terrain. Broad ridges and moor. Grass and heather slopes.

SKIING ABILITIES REQUIRED: Intermediate skills of ascent, traverse and descent. Any steep sections can be avoided. Ability to cover the distance

OTHER ABILITIES REQUIRED: Good winter navigation and hillcraft skills. Extra care approaching Carn nan Sac if visibility is poor.

SKIING EQUIPMENT NEEDED: General touring gear - steel edges if icy.

OTHER EQUIPMENT NEEDED: Full mountain equipment.

SNOW COVER: Very good. Enjoys a long season - usually good until April. Direct return route may involve some walking over easy ground in lean conditions. N-facing corrie between Carn a' Gheoidh and Carn nan Sac is particularly useful as it holds snow even after the nursery areas around Loch Vrotachan recede.

APPROACH ROADS: A93 Blairgowrie to Braemar. Parking at start point.

This is a good high level touring route to a fine viewpoint. The start point is at 650m above sea level which means skiable snow is quickly reached from the road and the route provides an option after snow has gone from lower hills. Although the tour begins at the bustling Glenshee downhill slopes the madding crowd is soon left behind as the route leads into an area which is lonely and remote, where no road penetrates and no habitated dwellings are to be found. As such it has been described as featureless, but in fact the route follows distinct natural features which assist navigation. It is well worth noting the lie of the snow on the outward route to assist route planning for the return. In particular cornicing on burns observed earlier in the day may be useful information later on.

From the car park ascend through the downhill skiing area to the

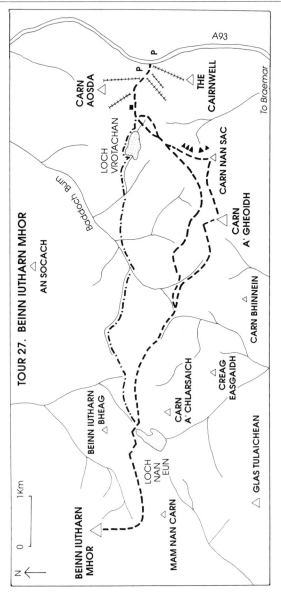

TOUR 27. BEINN IUTHARN MHOR

col between Carn Aosda and The Cairnwell above Loch Vrotachan. A rising traverse S and then SW leads up the N ridge of Carn nan Sac to a small cairn on its summit. Take care to avoid the steep cliffs on the SE flank of this ridge where cornices build up. There is an excellent snow bowl NW of Carn nan Sac which gives an accessible area for practice and "messing around" on skis. It is higher and less busy than the popular Loch Vrotachan. However the burn leading from this bowl to the Baddoch Burn does not always hold the snow well.

Continue W from Carn nan Sac until a short ascent leads to the summit of Carn a' Gheoidh, a mountain of Munro status. The best run from the summit goes briefly N along the E flank of the summit plateau and then turns W (approximately at 950m contour line).

There is excellent snow-holding in the N-flowing tributary of the Baddoch Burn or, if snow cover is complete, fine running along the ridge and down to open flanks following the line of the boundary indicated on the OS map. Gain the col at GR 089778 where snow may be thin late in the season.

Ascend NW the good snow bowl of the upper reaches of the Allt Elrig crossing the summit ridge of Carn a' Chlarsaich at a shallow col just below a pile of stones at the NE end of the ridge. Contour around the N flank of the ridge and descend gradually to Loch nan Eun. Ascend to the col between Mam nan Carn and Beinn Iutharn Bheag. From the col follow a rising traverse W, avoiding Mam nan Carn, to the col between it and Beinn Iutharn Mhor. Mam nan Carn can easily be included if wished on either the outward or return journey. Beinn Iutharn Bheag lies more off-route but is easy and accessible if skied from the col between it and Mam nan Carn.

From the col climb broad slopes N to the large and well constructed summit cairn of Beinn Iutharn Mhor. If visibility is good a panorama of mountains can be seen from here. Glas Tulaichean dominates the view S and shows itself to be an excellent snow-holding mountain. Beinn a' Ghlo, and the Glen Tilt hills, the Great Moss, the Cairngorms, sweep around to Lochnagar, Glas Maol and the hills of the Mounth.

For the descent follow the outward route to Loch nan Eun from where there is a choice of route depending on snow cover (observed earlier). If low-lying snow is poor follow the outward route over Carn a' Chlarsaich to the col at GR 089778. From here traverse E rising around the snow bowl of the tributary of the Baddoch Burn to the N

ridge of Carn a' Gheoidh and ascend this to the 900m contour. Note
that cornices may have built up above the burns at GR 102777 and GR
108772. Contour below Can nan Sac, where snow banks linger after
the crest of the ridge and the lower regions have lost their snow, to
gain the outward route and follow this back to the start point. This
route makes best use of diminishing snow, but requires clear weather.
Alternatively a more direct route leads back from Loch nan Eun, but
this may involve some walking if snow cover is poor. From the N end
of Loch nan Eun traverse ENE to the col beneath An Socach to where
a tributary of the Baddoch Burn cuts through the col at GR 080789.
Enter the obvious notch of the Baddoch Burn and follow it to the main
glen. In the upper reaches this may hold small cornices but lower
down it gives good sheltered running. Continue downstream to the
confluence at GR 103788 and traverse E around the ridge to the Loch
Vrotachan burns where snow should be found. Ascend to the loch
and the col above it to return to the start point.

28. GLENISLA FOREST

OS SHEET: 44 or 1:25,000 No.26/36

START POINT: Car park at entrance to the forest, Freuchies, GR
224608

TOTAL DISTANCE: 19.5kms   ASCENT: 350m

TIME: 5 hours 30 minutes. (Note: Racing skiers in the "Glenisla
March" will complete this in little more than one hour!).

TERRAIN: Forest roads and rides. Slopes of all gradients. Sections of
steep ascent and descent.

SKIING ABILITIES REQUIRED: Most of the route requires basic skills
only, so would suit skier of limited ability who may walk some
sections.

OTHER ABILITIES REQUIRED: Elementary map reading skills.
Ability to cover the distance on foot if not on ski.

SKIING EQUIPMENT NEEDED: Light touring gear.

OTHER EQUIPMENT NEEDED: Lightweight equipment/light rucksack.

SNOW COVER: A snow-holding forest, lying between 250m and

500m. Not unusual to drive unhopefully past green fields to reach the forest, yet find many kilometres of skiable snow preserved on the trails. Best snow-holding in the northern Glen Finlet and Glen Taitney sections. First few kilometres to beyond Tulloch frequently bare, thin or icy. Usual season December to March - but variable. Most tracks skiable with minimum cover - but not rides of tussocky grass.

APPROACH ROADS: B951 Kirriemuir to Glen Shee Road. 1km E of Kirkton of Glenisla turn N for East Mill Farm. Follow minor farm road over bridge to car parks at Freuchies.

Glenisla Forest has become one of the main centres in Britain for track skiing. The snow-holding properties of the forest have been long appreciated, and both the relative reliability of snow cover and the extent of skiable trails have prompted the forest to be chosen as the current venue for a number of officially recognised cross-country skiing races. These are usually held at the end of January/beginning of February.

A Nordic ski school has been established at nearby Knockshannoch Lodge. Tracks are sometimes machine-cut by the ski school, and there is a network of clearly marked and well maintained ski trails. These facilities, along with the publicity associated with the races, have increased public awareness of the area as a Nordic centre to such an extent that cross-country skiers converge on the forest in great numbers. On any weekend at peak season the area is crawling with them. A new car park at the entrance to the forest at Freuchies has been made to accommodate the numbers.

This popularity is due more to publicity than to the superior qualities of the forest over other forests for skiing. It is true that there are a lot of trails here suiting a range of abilities. But they are all approached along one route - from the car park to Tulloch. There is frequently poor snow cover on this section. It is busy, since it is where all skiers are funnelled. It is an uninspiring time-consuming approach to the snow. The trails themselves lead through uniform stances of cloned commercially planted conifers. There are few glimpses of surrounding country, which is desolate moorland anyway. The main features of the forest - its snow-holding and the extent of skiing available - will exhilarate the track skier and racer. But the ski-tourer, for whom what he is skiing through is as important as what he is skiing on, will find the forest lacking. There are many forests which

123

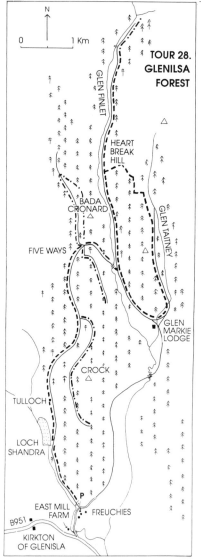

TOUR 28.
GLENILSA
FOREST

are more peaceful and beautiful than this.

Outwith the forest on the other hand, there is much to interest the ski-tourer. By following the forest trails N up Glen Finlet it is possible to ascend N towards Broom Hill and Bawhelps. Broad slopes and the excellent langlauf terrain stretching to the N of Mayar can be accessed. From upper Glen Isla, to the W of the forest, routes from the end of the public road, GR 192697, can be followed NE to Finalty Hill or NW via Glen Brighty and Little Glas Maol to the Glas Maol Plateau. If skiing out of the forest heavier skiing equipment - general touring or mountain touring gear is required.

It is worth noting that the road from Freuchies to Glenmarkie Lodge is not suitable for skiing and is not part of the trail system. It is used by vehicles which destroy the snow cover, and the verges are drainage ditches or very narrow. The road is open and exposed and does not collect or preserve snow as do the forest trails.

The route described here is of course only one of many

trail options within the forest. The current OS 1,25,000 series map of the area gives a fairly accurate indication of roads and rides, most of which are skiable, (although some rides have a difficult base of tussock grass). Waymarkers point the way to routes giving good skiing. This tour follows some of the route of the prestigious race the "Glenisla March" and although it is quite long it can be shortened easily.

From the car park enter the forest and ski NW past Loch Shandra to the stiff uphill pull (often icy) by the prominent cottage at Tulloch. The slopes around Loch Shandra are often used as nursery slopes. As the forest road turns away from the open area snow cover improves and the gradient eases to give good track skiing to the main junction, GR 225657, 5.5kms from the start point. This junction is known as "Five Ways", but in fact six rides, roads and routes meet here. (See below)

Continue E along the main forest road, which descends rapidly to the bridge over Finlet Burn. E of the bridge a waymarked road leads up Glen Finlet. This is an excellent snow-holding route and can be followed N for over 5kms, ascending at a pleasant angle to within reach of the forest edge. It gives a fine running descent. Rides ascend E from the road towards the crest of the ridge between Glen Finlet and Glen Taitney. They give varied and testing skiing between the forest roads in each of the two glens.

This route continues up Glen Finlet to one such ride, which has been aptly named "Heart Break Hill". This begins 2kms from the junction, GR 230673, where a fence leads up the hillside separating trees of different ages. It is waymarked, and at the time of writing a small yellow hut is to be found where it meets the road. It is a steep bank, skiable for those with herringbone skills of ascent.

"Heart Break Hill" leads to the edge of the trees, where snow-holding is good. Following a waymarked route turn SSE along the edge of the forest to a track leading S back into the trees. Follow this for 250m distance to reach a crossroads of routes. Turn E (left) and descend following the track as it bends sharply S and then descends gently to the forest road in Glen Taitney.

The forest road ascending Glen Taitney from Glenmarkie Lodge is also a good snow-holding route. It terminates 2.5kms N of the lodge, but rides can be followed to the forest boundary from where it ends. It is to this road that the route leads, joining it just S of its termination point. The route follows the Glen Taitney road back towards the lodge.

Keeping N of the lodge follow the broad forest road W then NW back to the Glen Finlet trails and the bridge over the Finlet Burn. Follow the outward route back to "Five Ways" and hence back to the start point.

From "Five Ways" there are two short excursions of note. One leads N to give a 3km circuit, usually skied anticlockwise. Take the trail which ascends stiffly N towards Bada Crionard. Continue N for almost 1km to fence posts, then bear left (NW) along a ride. This appears to end, but turns sharply left downhill for a short steep run to a forest track. Turn S onto the track which returns to "Five Ways".

The second route runs S from "Five Ways", ascending steeply at first, then contouring around Craigie Law. This route holds the snow, and sometimes snow can be found here when there is inferior cover in other parts of the forest.

There is a track which runs for 2kms along the W flank of Crock parallel to the forest road from Loch Shandra to "Five Ways". It gives good skiing along its length, but ends abruptly. It can be accessed from a point half-way between Tulloch and "Five Ways" at GR 224644, where currently a cleared area adjoins the forest. There is a vehicle turning area here, and the track is reached by ascending E up the edge of the trees.

29. GLENDOLL FOREST

OS SHEET: 44   START POINT: Picnic Place and Car Park, Glen Doll, GR 284762

TOTAL DISTANCE: 4kms   ASCENT: 70m   TIME: 1 hours 10 minutes

TERRAIN: Forest roads and paths. One steep section - can be avoided.

SKIING ABILITIES REQUIRED: Suit beginner.

OTHER ABILITIES REQUIRED: Elementary map reading skills.

SKIING EQUIPMENT NEEDED: Light touring gear.

OTHER EQUIPMENT NEEDED: Lightweight equipment.

SNOW COVER: This is a low level tour (land lies between 250m and 300m above sea level) and hence snow cover is dependent upon a fall of snow in the glens. However a combination of several factors often makes snow cover here good enough to ski on during the winter months.

Firstly, the location on the E side of the country means the forest lies in the path of the cold and snow-bearing NE winds, secondly the shade of the forest preserves the snow that does fall, and thirdly the tracks are skiable with only a thin covering of snow.

APPROACH ROADS: From Kirriemuir B955 to Clova Hotel, then minor road up Glen Clova. Parking at start point.

Glendoll Forest is a small forest, of little import to mountaineers who scamper through it on their way to nearby mighty Munros and craggy corries. However, it is a delightful place to explore on skis. In comparative safety from the winter storms on the surrounding highlands the Nordic Skier is treated to picturesque forest and riverside scenery, views to the ragged heights above, and amused by the rise and fall of the trail. All the forest tracks can be skied in a few hours. Many of them come to a dead halt, which means retreat is back the way you came. However, the trails are broad and well defined and it is not unusual to find others have been there before, and made tracks.

The little tour chosen is a gem. It is short, but there are several places where it can be extended by exploring at will sidetracks and trails. The skiing is never difficult, but small sections of steep slope or

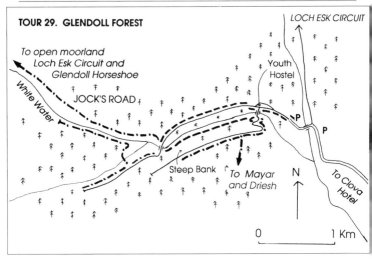

natural obstacles demand attention and make it fun.

From the picnic place take the forest road leading W into Glendoll Forest. Follow the track leading below the youth hostel, and keeping N of the river ski easily to a well-marked junction, where Jock's Road leads away to the right. Jock's Road heads through the trees for another 2.5kms before exiting to open moorland, and makes for a pleasant side jaunt, but the main tour descends to cross a wide bridge over White Water. The forest road continues W for a kilometre, and both it and its offshoots provide further exploratory skiing, but the main tour does a "U" turn and heads back to the start point along a path on the S bank of the river.

Shortly a bridge across a small burn is reached. Immediately after this there is an interesting option on the right. A steep bank leads up to a forest road. This bank gives entertaining skiing in descent. The forest road at the top of the bank can be followed down to join the tour further downstream. Turn left at the top of the bank if you wish to return this way. However this option is not as attractive as the lovely little trail along the aptly named White Water.

Follow the path and the river until a junction is reached, whereupon there is a choice of following the river along a good path, or bearing right to join the broad forest road leading down gently to a gate and the bridge over White Water. This is the forest road which leads along the top of the steep bank.

Cross the bridge to rejoin the outward route and retrace your tracks back to the start point.

30. THE GLEN DOLL HORSESHOE

OS SHEET: 44

START POINT: Picnic Place and Car Park, Glen Doll, GR 284762

TOTAL DISTANCE: 23kms   ASCENT: 1040m   TIME: 7 hours 30 minutes

TERRAIN: Forest trail and track leading to gently undulating moorland plateau.

SKIING ABILITIES REQUIRED: For majority of route diagonal stride, snowplough and traverse repertoire will suffice. Two sections require skill ascending/descending steep and rock-strewn terrain - nervous skiers can walk these sections. Ability to ski the distance.

OTHER ABILITIES REQUIRED: Excellent winter navigation and hillcraft skills and good general fitness.

SKIING EQUIPMENT NEEDED: Full mountain equipment.

OTHER EQUIPMENT NEEDED: Full mountain equipment.

SNOW COVER: Generally good, although summits may be blown clear. Plateau still good in late season. Although low lying (250m at start) the forest holds the snow well.

APPROACH ROADS: From Kirriemuir B955 to Clova Hotel, then minor road up Glen Clova. Parking at start point.

A high level tour offering many kilometres of easy skiing, three Munro Summits and one Top, and the opportunity to dash up Driesh.

Take the forest road leading W past Glendoll Youth Hostel to a bridge across White Water. Cross the bridge and wind up the hillside on a broad forest road for approximately 1km before striking left (SW) and steeply up a narrow forest trail. (Returning this way requires great concentration.) Upon emerging from the forest take the line of the footpath traversing the steep Shank of Drumfollow. This is difficult to ski and prone to icing. There is usually better snow

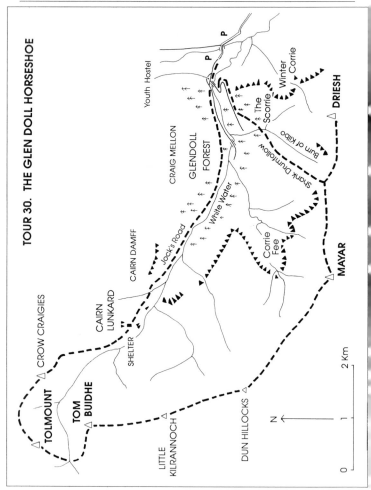

TOUR 30. THE GLEN DOLL HORSESHOE

lying along the course of the Burn of Kilbo, but a dauntingly steep exit up to the col. It may be worth utilising the snow in the burn and then backtracking in long ascending zig-zags to regain the line of the path. Or just walk.

From the col the ascent of Driesh adds 3kms (return to the col) and 200m of height gain to the tour. The first half kilometre from the col is steep. (Fence posts)

Mayar lies 1.5kms easy skiing W of the col. Fence posts along the route aid navigation.

Descend Mayar on its broad NW flank and reach Tom Buidhe via Dun Hillocks and Little Kilrannoch (bypass on its W flank). 6kms and only 180m of ascent! In bad conditions do not try to escape E into Glen Doll via the easy-looking slopes of Fee Burn or Dun Hillocks. They steepen into a vicious cliff line. Either retreat via the route of ascent or continue to safe routes into Glen Doll N of the cliffs. A burn-filled valley separates Tom Buidhe from Tolmount, and the shrewd skier will descend Tom Buidhe on its NW side and strike up the SW ridge of Tolmount, in an arc which utilises the least amount of unnecessary descent and reascent.

The burns flowing from Tolmount into Glen Doll offer very easy slopes for the less able/tired skier to return by. However to include Crow Craigies only demands another 40m of gentle climbing and basic skill in traversing to descend safely to the shelter below Cairn Lunkard. If the burn is skied leave it at the height of the shelter. It tumbles over a series of falls below this point.

The shelter may be completely snowed over. It is not unusual for skiers to ski over the roof without realising it. It is in reasonable condition and can be a life-saver in bad weather.

The next 2kms below the shelter are difficult. Take care. The route is barred by a series of rock outcrops and basins and is boulder-strewn and steep. There is a path somewhere under the snow! Keep well back from the burn. However once over this tricky section, the forest is reached and a good track leads the skier safely down predominantly gentle gradients (with occasional short "fun" sections) along the route of Jock's Road to a broad forest road and a final 1.5kms easy track past the youth hostel back to the car park.

31. LOCH ESK CIRCUIT, GLEN CLOVA

OS SHEET: 44   START POINT: Picnic Place and Car Park, GR 284762

TOTAL DISTANCE: 16kms   ASCENT: 600m   TIME: 5 hours

TERRAIN: Land-Rover and forest tracks and open moorland.

SKIING ABILITIES REQUIRED: Generally easy skiing requiring elementary diagonal stride, climbing, snowplough, traverse and kick turn. Stick brake may be useful descending Jock's Road. One section of difficult skiing may be walked.

OTHER ABILITIES REQUIRED: Basic winter navigation and hillcraft skills.

SKIING EQUIPMENT NEEDED: General touring gear.

OTHER EQUIPMENT NEEDED: Full mountain equipment.

SNOW COVER: The first part of the route is low lying and needs good overall snow cover to be skiable. However from Bachnagairn the burns and gentle slopes collect and hold snow. The shelter and shade of the Glendoll Forest mean the tracks here hold the snow after thaw elsewhere.

APPROACH ROADS: From Kirriemuir B955 to Clova Hotel, then minor road up Glen Clova. Parking at the start point.

A pleasant round trip linking Glen Clova and Glen Doll. Best saved for days when the snow is low-lying.

Follow the Land-Rover track heading N up Glen Clova, without climbing any real height until after the first hour. Continue up the course of the river, through the shelter of an open larch wood at Bachnagairn, to the confluence with the Burn of Gowal.

From here Broad Cairn can be skied quite easily, by following the Burn of Gowal and then striking E to the summit. This ascent involves a further 2kms and 350m of height gain.

Turn SW away from the valley floor and climb easily the broad heather slope leading to the flat area of Loch Esk. Still climbing, continue past Loch Esk in the same direction up the line of the burn to a broad col N of Cairn Lunkard. It is advisable, particularly in poor visibility to continue on the same bearing to descend into Glen Doll N of the shelter. The slope is steep if taken directly - but is broad and

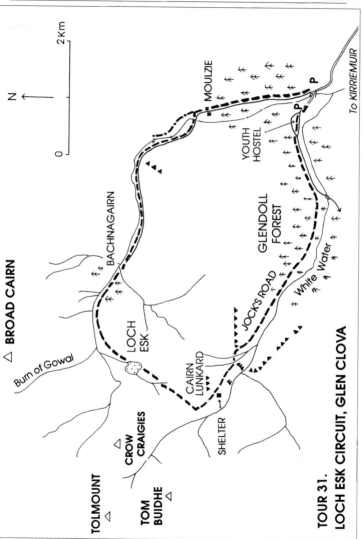

△ BROAD CAIRN

TOLMOUNT △

TOM
BUIDHE △

CROW
CRAIGIES △

Burn of Gowal

LOCH
ESK

BACHNAGAIRN

CAIRN
LUNKARD

SHELTER

JOCK'S ROAD

GLENDOLL
FOREST

White Water

MOULZIE

YOUTH
HOSTEL

P
P
P

To KIRRIEMUIR

N ←

0   2 Km

TOUR 31.
LOCH ESK CIRCUIT, GLEN CLOVA

133

so enables the more nervous to traverse and kick turn. However if the skier chooses a more southerly direction to bring him into Glen Doll below the shelter he must be prepared to encounter tricky terrain of small rocky cliff lines and steep restricted skiing.

The shelter is a memorial to a party who lost their lives in these hills - it may be completely buried and not easy to find. From the shelter the route is as for the Glen Doll Horseshoe Tour, (Tour 30).

The 2kms below the shelter are steep, stepped and difficult. Keep away from the river. In contrast the final 4kms through the forest are a delightful romp, often enhanced by being able to use the tracks made by other skiers earlier in the day. Join the main forest track and ski past the youth hostel to the car park.

32. GREEN HILL, GLEN CLOVA

OS SHEET: 44   START POINT: The Clova Hotel, GR 327732

TOTAL DISTANCE: 16kms   ASCENT: 830m   TIME: 5 hours 30 minutes

TERRAIN: Snow-filled burns, gently undulating moorland plateau. One steeper, but broad slope to descend.

SKIING ABILITIES REQUIRED: Generally easy slopes requiring elementary diagonal stride, climbing skills, snowplough, traverse and kick turn.

OTHER ABILITIES REQUIRED: Basic winter navigation and hillcraft skills.

SKIING EQUIPMENT NEEDED: General touring gear - steel edges if icy.

OTHER EQUIPMENT NEEDED: Light rucksack/Full mountain equipment.

SNOW COVER: Burns and corries have excellent snow-holding properties. Even when snow has left the surrounding moorland it lingers here.

APPROACH ROADS: B955 from Kirriemuir.

The moorland plateau N of Green Hill offers superb cross-country terrain. Snow-holding is unexpectedly good, for snow is blown into

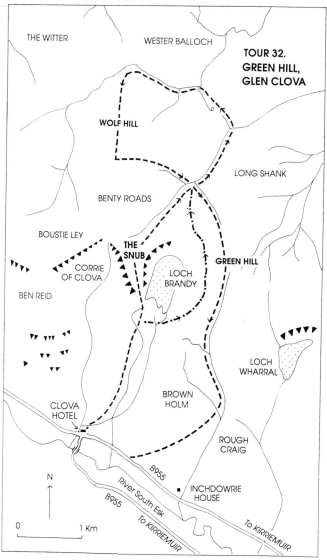

TOUR 32.
GREEN HILL,
GLEN CLOVA

THE WITTER

WESTER BALLOCH

WOLF HILL

LONG SHANK

BENTY ROADS

BOUSTIE LEY

THE SNUB

GREEN HILL

CORRIE OF CLOVA

LOCH BRANDY

BEN REID

LOCH WHARRAL

CLOVA HOTEL

BROWN HOLM

ROUGH CRAIG

N

INCHDOWRIE HOUSE

B955

River South Esk

B955

TO KIRRIEMUIR

TO KIRRIEMUIR

0   1 Km

Ideal nordic touring terrain, Green Hill, Glen Clova.
Looking NW to Meikle Pap, Lochnagar and the White Mounth

Telemark descent from Green Hill to Glen Clova

the shallow-sided burns, and skiable routes along "corridors" of snow are created. Even if as you set off from the glen it appears that there is no hope of snow, it is quite common to be surprised to find kilometres of snow lying in ribbons along the burns. There is a wealth of uncomplicated downhill runs - a delight to ski. Lengthy routes lead N to Mount Keen and Deeside, W to Capel Mounth and E to Glen Lee and Glen Esk over gentle, grassy (sometimes boggy) moor extending for kilometres about the 600m contour line. This is terrain to cheer the skier - but it will not inspire the hillwalker.

This short circuit is a good introduction to the area. It follows a route usually skiable when snow cover elsewhere is poor and includes a fine run S from Green Hill.

Climb steeply the path behind the hotel in the direction of Loch Brandy. (No brandy!) The burn to the right of the track may be holding snow, however if the snowline is high it is probably more efficient to walk briskly all the way to the top of The Snub before donning skis. This tactic gets you smartly to "good space" snow and the enjoyable downhill runs. However if you are keen to ski as soon as you can the corrie slopes S of Green Hill often hold snow and offer an easy ascent and are reached by traversing below Loch Brandy, and crossing a low ridge.

From The Snub descend the Burn of Longshank to the confluence at GR 349778. Turn NNW into a wide gap and ski easily to the confluence at GR 344784. From here follow W into a much narrower and steep-sided gap. Once in this narrow gap either ascend directly to Wolf Hill or take an easier gradient by traversing anticlockwise upwards around Wolf Hill, ascending gradually to the broad summit.

Descend Wolf Hill to the confluence at GR 344769 and cross the route of earlier. A gentle ascent to the summit of Green Hill marks the last climb of the tour.

From Green Hill descend S into the broad corrie. The start of this descent is steep - the crux of the tour. However the less able should survive with long traverses and kick turns. The burn leading down to Inchdowrie presents a narrow finger of snow, daring to extend far below the general snowline. Take care snow bridges do not collapse. From the end of the snow walk back to the B955.

33. MOUNT KEEN

OS SHEET: **44**

START POINT: Car Park just E of end of public road, Glen Esk, GR 447804

TOTAL DISTANCE: 25kms   ASCENT: 860m   TIME: 7 hours 40 minutes

TERRAIN: Hill tracks leading to undulating plateau. One section of steep track. Moorland slopes, steep in places, but broad and spacious.

SKIING ABILITIES REQUIRED: Skills for ascending and descending broad open slopes of all gradients.

OTHER ABILITIES REQUIRED: Basic/Good winter navigation and hillcraft skills.

SKIING EQUIPMENT NEEDED: Mountain touring gear.

OTHER EQUIPMENT NEEDED: Full mountain equipment.

SNOW COVER: Well placed to receive snow from snow-bearing E winds. Snow holds well on the hill tracks - often a ribbon of snow lingers here after thaw on surrounding moor. Long approach to the snow-holding area, but walking speeded by excellent hill tracks.

APPROACH ROADS: Minor road up Glen Esk from Edzell.

The sleek cone of Mount Keen crowns a massive wasteland of superb Nordic touring terrain. The summit slopes rise from an expanse of gently undulating plateau, dissected by snow-holding burns. This is an attractive hill for walkers, since the Mounth Road leads almost to the summit and approaches from delightful and beautiful glens - Glen Tanar in the N, Glen Mark in the S. For skiers there is the additional attraction that a wealth of lengthy ski routes radiate from the summit across the surrounding terrain. It is the exploration of these that is the joy of Nordic touring, rather than the simple summit ascent. Indeed the attraction of the Mount Keen area to skiers was known to the very earliest of Scottish ski-runners. In one of the first recorded mountain ski ascents in Scotland on 15 March 1909 a party ascended the mountain from Ballater. That day skisters donned skis at the hotel door and skied the whole route, some 15 miles to the summit and back, without having to carry skis on any section.

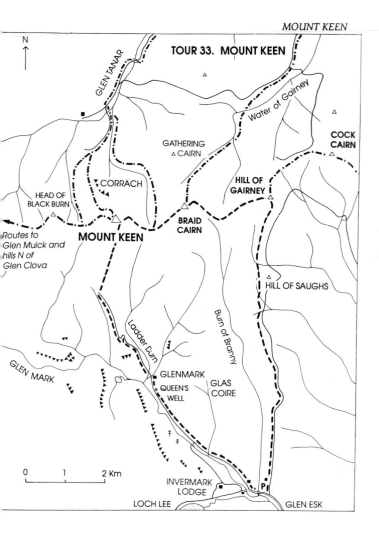

N

TOUR 33. MOUNT KEEN

GLEN TANAR

Water of Gairney

COCK CAIRN

GATHERING △ CAIRN

CORRACH

HILL OF GAIRNEY

HEAD OF BLACK BURN

BRAID CAIRN

MOUNT KEEN

Routes to Glen Muick and hills N of Glen Clova

HILL OF SAUGHS

GLEN MARK

Ladder Burn

Burn of Branny

GLENMARK

GLAS COIRE

QUEEN'S WELL

0   1   2 Km

INVERMARK LODGE

P

LOCH LEE

GLEN ESK

Mount Keen is the most easterly of Munro Summits, and is well placed to receive snow from snow-bearing E winds. However, the surrounding plateau undulates at a lower level and has a shorter season than the other more popular Cairngorm plateaux to the W.

The most rewarding expeditions traverse the area from glen to glen. However, this requires transport arrangements beyond the organisation of most. The circuit described here from Glen Esk gives a satisfying ski route across the hills to the E of Mount Keen, utilising some of the excellent hill tracks of the area for quick access to the snow.

The route starts at the end of the public road up Glen Esk and follows the public footpath up the NE side of Glen Mark past the Queen's Well to Glenmark Cottage. The track continues N, up Ladder Burn, and leads steeply by a series of zig-zags up the W bank to the shoulder of Mount Keen, from where the original Mounth Road passes to the W of the summit cone. The summit can be approached by the S ridge, or from the E or W flank, depending on snow cover. The angle of slope steepens, but the flanks are so broad that the final ascent should present no undue complications.

The summit is a fine viewpoint offering extensive views in all directions. The route goes E to Braid Cairn and then to Hill of Gairney. The E flanks of both Mount Keen and Braid Cairn are fairly steep, but are broad enough to allow long descending traverses, and have easy run-outs to flat cols. From Hill of Gairney a hill track leads S and crosses open moorland and easy slopes, returning to Glen Esk just E of the start point.

Alternatives

1. Returning to Glen Esk

Returning directly to Glen Esk from Mount Keen involves avoiding the steep sides of the Ladder Burn and Upper Glen Mark. It is possible to go E to Braid Cairn, and then S, keeping either between Easter Burn and Burn of Branny to Glas Coire, or between Easter Burn and Ladder Burn to the spur of Pandewen and then via a steep descent to Glenmark.

There is a steep, but skiable run down the slopes of the burn W of Couternach to the Water of Mark for skiers with advanced downhill technique.

2. E from Hill of Gairney

From Hill of Gairney the superb plateau terrain undulates E to Cock Cairn, Hill of Cat and Tampie, and then beyond the pass used by the Mounth Tracks to Mudlee Bracks, Hill of Cammie and the elevated Mount Battock. In addition to the Firmounth and Fungle roads there is a wealth of tracks leading N to Glen Tanar and Deeside, and S to Glen Esk giving speedy access to the skiing grounds and a proliferation of routes within the area.

3. N to Glen Tanar

It is popular to approach Mount Keen from the N via Glen Tanar. This is a delightful glen and it is easy to understand its popularity. The Forest of Glen Tanar is natural pine forest, and is served by excellent, well-graded tracks. The Mounth Road which passes so close to the summit of Mount Keen passes along it. The approach is a lengthy one, (13kms from the small car park behind Glen Tanar House to the summit) much of it will for the most part be snow-free. However if there is snow in the glen this is the finest route to the mountain. Descending back into the glen note the crags of Corrach N of the summit. From the hills to the E of Mount Keen (Braid Cairn and Gathering Cairn, Hill of Gairney and Cock Cairn), snow-holding, N-facing slopes, and gentle runs along the burns feeding Water of Gairney give good running. A useful hill track E of Clachan Yell descends to the forest and the Water of Tanar.

4. W from Mount Keen

W of Mount Keen a wasteland of confusing featureless plateau levels above the 600m contour line allowing lengthy routes suited to langlauf skis. An ascent from the road in Glen Muick is possible via a number of broad spurs which carry hill tracks. Alternatively turning S at Fasheilach a line along the watershed leads to Black Hill of Mark and then via the Lair of Aldararie or Wolf Hill and Green Hill to Glen Clova. From Glen Clova to the summit of Mount Keen a route of some 18kms can be skied along snow-holding burns and over broad undistinguished rises with only the first 2kms of ascent from the glen being below the 600m contour line, and with most of the route gently undulating between the 650m and the 750m contour lines. The route goes N from Benty Roads to Fasheilach and then E to Mount Keen.

DRUMOCHTER

Travelling through the Pass of Drumochter there appears little evidence of the pleasure of this area for ski touring. The Pass is a gloomy place, intruded by the A9, the railway and an ugly line of pylons. However it is the case that the hills on both sides offer some excellent touring with fine views of the surrounding mountains and thrilling descents. The hills E of Drumochter are particularly suited to Nordic mountain touring.

Before the development of uplift facilities for downhill skiing at other sites in Scotland the gullies above the Pass of Drumochter were often used by downhill skiers, and at the time of writing there are plans to install uplift facilities in the area.

The road reaches a height of 462m above sea level and there is sometimes skiable snow available without having to walk far from the car (or the train). Although the Pass is prone to blocking by wind-blown snow, the authorities recognise this route as the main access to the N and it is kept open whenever practically possible.

THE EAST DRUMOCHTER HILLS

Hidden above the steep banks rising from the Pass there is a high level plateau, with easy undulation and miles of excellent langlauf potential. This is grassy terrain and does not need a thick covering of snow to be skiable. In windy weather the grass helps to bind the snow, and there is sometimes skiing possible here when the stony tundra plateaux have been blown clear. The ridges and gullies rising from the Pass to the plateau face a variety of directions from NNW through W to SSW. Thus there is an abundance of N-facing slopes and a good chance of snow on one or other slope somewhere above the Pass. There are several routes up to the plateau, and for the descent back down. The choice depends on snow cover, skiing ability, weather, time available and whether one needs to return to the start point for transport home. The tour described returns to the start point and uses terrain well suited to Nordic equipment.

34. THE EAST DRUMOCHTER HILLS

OS SHEET: 42   START POINT: Lay-by on E side of A9 at GR 631763
TOTAL DISTANCE: 17kms   ASCENT: 750m   TIME: 5 hours 30 minutes

TERRAIN: Short climb up steep heathery bank leads to wide easy gully and then open grassy high level plateau.

SKIING ABILITIES REQUIRED: Mostly easy slopes requiring basic climbing, traversing and descent techniques.

OTHER ABILITIES REQUIRED: Excellent winter navigation and hillcraft skills.

SKIING EQUIPMENT NEEDED: General touring gear, but steel edges necessary if icy.

OTHER EQUIPMENT NEEDED: Full mountain equipment.

SNOW COVER: Very good. Enjoys a long season. Especially good in early season or lean spells as the grassy terrain is skiable with minimum cover.

APPROACH ROADS: A9 through Pass of Drumochter.

This is a tour across ideal touring terrain with some fine descents, extensive views and including the ascent of two mountains of Munro status.

The point of start depends on whether snow is lying at road level or not. Most usually it is not, and the quickest way to the snow is to climb steeply on foot the heathery banks above the road, just N of the boundary between Tayside Region and Highland Region. If there is snow lying an easier angled ascent can be made from the road at GR 637746 NE up a shallow burn for almost 1km to flat ground. Turn N for a further 1km and gain the broad ridge and fence posts leading towards Meall a' Chaorainn.

The route ascends Jean's Gully, an easy angled, shallow gully running SW of Meall a' Chaorainn. Despite its sun-facing aspect it has long been known to hold skiable snow and before the development of uplift facilities elsewhere, it was in favour as a downhill nursery area. It is indeed a pleasant place to ski on a sunny day, when there are fine views of the mountains W of Drumochter. From the top

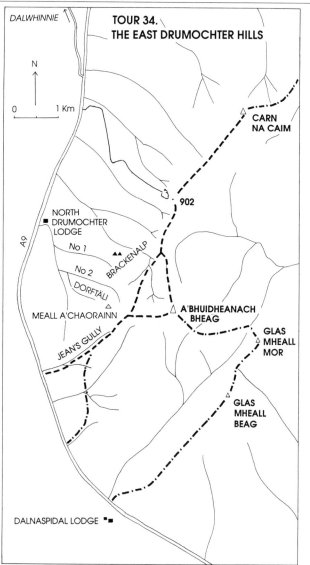

DALWHINNIE

TOUR 34.
THE EAST DRUMOCHTER HILLS

N

0   1 Km

CARN
NA CAIM

902

NORTH
DRUMOCHTER
LODGE

A9

No 1

No 2

BRACKENALP

DORFTÄLI

MEALL A'CHAORAINN

A'BHUIDHEANACH
BHEAG

GLAS
MHEALL
MOR

JEAN'S GULLY

GLAS
MHEALL
BEAG

DALNASPIDAL LODGE

At the top of Jean's Gully looking W over The Pass of Drumochter to Sgairneach Mhor, Beinn Udlamain, and A' Mharconaich

of the gully many near and distant mountains come into view, the Loch Garry Gap allowing a sighting of Ben More and Stob Binnean 60kms to the SW

At the top of the gully the fence posts lead E and can be followed over easy langlauf terrain to the Ordnance Survey column on the summit of A' Bhuidheanach Bheag (pronounced "Bunny-ach-beg"). This mountain appears first in the alphabet of Munros, but last in the list of spectacular summits. It is little more than a rise in surrounding bald terrain. However it is easy to ascend on skis and a worthwhile viewpoint.

From the summit the route crosses the plateau to Carn na Caim, 5kms to the N. The fence posts lead that way too and are an invaluable help to navigation if visibility deteriorates. However in good visibility one is permitted the luxury of choosing the best route for the day's snow, which may or may not be by the fence posts. The descent N from A' Bhuidheanach Bheag is very pleasant and the bealach between A' Bhuidheanach Bheag and A' Bhuidheanach has some shelter. In late season the snow tends to lie on the E-facing slopes of the plateau.

The fence posts lead close but not all the way to the summit of Carn na Caim. They turn SE just S of the summit. This is so flat that the highest point is not obvious although at the time of writing a low cairn with a protruding stake marks the recognised high point.

There is vast ski touring potential from here, and if transport at Cuaich can be arranged it is worth considering an exploration of the rolling plateau to the NE. However if a return to the start point is necessary the outward route is retraced to the bealach between A' Bhuidheanach and A' Bhuidheanach Bheag, from where an easy ascent of the upper reaches of the Allt Coire Chuirn leads SW to the top of Jean's Gully just SE of Meall a' Chaorainn. The outward route is descended, Jean's Gully giving easy skiing on wide and gentle slopes, until it steepens and becomes difficult for skiing below the 650m contour line.

Alternatives

1. Glas Mheall Mor

From A' Bhuidheanach Bheag easy terrain leads ESE to the summit cone of Glas Mheall Mor (2kms). Note cornices sometimes present problems just NW of the summit in the gullies draining SW to the Allt Coire Mhic-sith and NE to the Cama' Choire. In poor visibility navigation to find the narrow neck between these two gullies can be extremely difficult over the vast expanse of featureless snowy terrain from A' Bhuidheanach Bheag. In such conditions it is better to aim a few hundred metres NE of this neck.

To ascend from the road, the NW slope facing the Allt Coire Mhic-sith holds snow better than the S-facing flanks of Glas Mheall Beag. A long and steady ascent climbs this steep bank to the col N of Glas Mheall Beag, or to include Glas Mheall Beag the ridge of Druim Coire Mhic-sith gives an easy approach and a fine descent of the snow-holding NE flank.

2. Ascents / Descents to the Plateau

The gullies above the Pass give a wide choice of routes of varying difficulty to and from the plateau. A study of the map reveals those with snow-holding N-facing slopes and the all important gradient.

Snow cover for some can be checked from the road and the best route to suit the skier and the day thus chosen. Just N of the Pass a bulldozed track climbs the hillside to a disused quarry and is well used as an easy angled and obvious route of ascent. However, it is not recommended in descent, the slopes to the N offering less restricted skiing. The Brackenalp gives interesting skiing on easy, snow-holding terrain. This is the gentle slope NW of the circular contour between Meall a' Chaorainn and the steep cleft of the Allt Coire Chuirn. It is named after Bill Bracken, whose ski schools once used the nursery slopes hereabouts. The gully descending from here to join the Allt Coire Dubhaig is known as No.1 Gully. It is pleasantly angled and collects snow.

The NW flank of Meall a' Chaorainn gives some very steep skiing which enjoyed popularity among downhill skiers in the past. The Dorftali is a steep run down the gully central to this slope, and gives extreme skiing for those with fully paid insurance policies. No.2 Gully curves around from just NE of Meall A' Chaorainn but is generally too confined to give good skiing.

From Carn na Caim it is possible to descend the snow-holding slopes to the N of the Allt Coire Uilleim. The ridges trending N from this summit give excellent terrain for Nordic touring and the corries enclosed within them hold snow late into the season. Snow cover here can be seen from the A9 N of the Pass.

35. THE WEST DRUMOCHTER HILLS

OS SHEET: 42   START POINT: Lay-by on W side of A9 at GR 632756

TOTAL DISTANCE: 14kms   ASCENT: 840m   TIME: 5 hours

TERRAIN: Mountain slopes of all gradients.

SKIING ABILITIES REQUIRED: Ability to ski steep slopes and cope with difficult snow conditions. The skiing is restricted in places.

OTHER ABILITIES REQUIRED: Excellent winter navigation and hillcraft skills. Good judgement of snow slopes.

SKIING EQUIPMENT NEEDED: Mountain touring gear - skins.

OTHER EQUIPMENT NEEDED: Full mountain equipment.

SNOW COVER: Good. Enjoys a long season. Crests of ridges may blow clear. Best cover on Sgairneach Mhor. Snow line can be confirmed from the A9 at the start point.

APPROACH ROADS: A9 through Pass of Drumochter.

W of the Pass of Drumochter lie four Munro Summits which can be traversed by a fit party in a day's skiing. The tour describes a circuit of three of them, which lie conveniently in horseshoe formation around Coire Dhomhain. Geal-charn lies to the N and can be included as an extension to the main tour. Generally speaking it does not hold the snow as well as the others.

These are very accessible mountains, popular because if snow is lying high it can quickly be reached from the Pass at 462m above sea level. It is a challenging mountain tour with outstanding views and some excellent downhill running. The running is good in both directions, so the direction of the wind on the day will probably determine which way round it is skied. It is described here in the clockwise direction.

From the A9 descend to ruined buildings and cross the railway line (little warning of oncoming trains). Gain the good track up Coire Dhomhain and ascend SW the broad and easy slope to gain the NE ridge of Sgairneach Mhor. Crossing the Allt Coire Dhomhain is a problem when in spate. There are fine views into the wide Coire Creagach, where impressive cornices build up. Ascend the crest of the ridge - keeping back from the corniced N side - to reach an OS

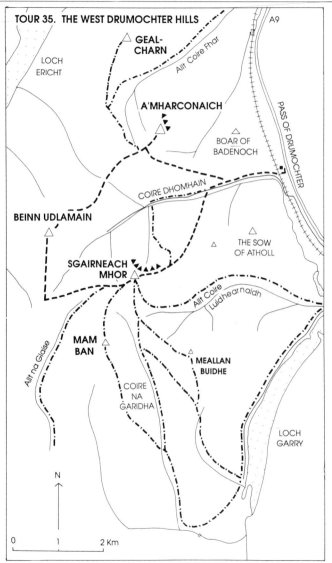

TOUR 35. THE WEST DRUMOCHTER HILLS

A9

△ GEAL-CHARN

LOCH ERICHT

Allt Coire Fhar

A'MHARCONAICH △▶

PASS OF DRUMOCHTER

△ BOAR OF BADENOCH

COIRE DHOMHAIN

BEINN UDLAMAIN

△ THE SOW OF ATHOLL

△

SGAIRNEACH MHOR ▶▶▶△

Allt Coire Luidhearnaidh

Allt na Glaise

MAM BAN △

△ MEALLAN BUIDHE

COIRE NA GARIDHA

LOCH GARRY

N ↑

0   1   2 Km

Looking W to Ben Alder from the summit of Sgairneach Mhor

*Looking SW into Coire Creagach, on the ascent from
Coire Dhomhain to Sgairneach Mhor,*

column on the summit plateau of Sgairneach Mhor. This is a good
viewpoint of mountains in all directions.

Sgairneach Mhor is the best ski mountain on the tour. It has good
snow-holding and broad easy flanks on all but the N side. It makes

a fine destination in itself, with ideal Nordic terrain inviting exploration to the S - see alternatives. Throughout the ascent and from the summit the character of the hills on the far side of the Allt Coire Dhomhain can be seen. In particular, note should be taken of any cornicing or signs of avalanche. Later in the season the best ribbons of snow for the descent can be spotted.

The route descends the wide and easy W slopes of Sgairneach Mhor to a broad col at the head of the Allt Coire Dhomhain. This area holds snow particularly well, and the run is one of the highlights of the tour.

Ascend the ridge leading to Beinn Udlamain. A line of fence posts follows the crest to the summit cairn. The ridge is bouldery and may be blown clear in places. There is a feeling of exposure and height, accentuated by the steepness of the flanks on each side. There are also excellent views to Ben Alder, improving with the ascent. Beinn Udlamain is one of the best places from which to view this complex and elusive mountain group.

The route continues NE along a whaleback ridge leading after 3.5kms to A' Mharconaich. This is a high level traverse with fine mountain views. The crest of the ridge may be blown clear, in which case snow on either side can be followed. The line of fence posts leads intermittently along the ridge, but descends SE 0.5kms before the summit. The summit is flat and rock-shattered but falls away steeply to the E where cornices build up.

The N flanks of A' Mharconaich hold the snow, and if Geal-charn is to be included in the tour they are descended to the col at the head of the Allt Coire Fhar. The best run down begins W of the summit and follows the snow-holding line of a shallow depression containing the most W tributary of the Allt Coire Fhar. The ridge ahead is then ascended to reach the summit of Geal-charn. The ridge may be blown clear, in which case snow must be sought below the crest. The tall cairns which mark this mountain to travellers on the A9, are not at the summit, but lie on a shoulder to the E. It is possible to descend to the A9 at Balsporran Cottages. However the easy angled and N-facing slopes descending to the Allt Beul an Sporain gives false promise. They do not hold the snow and deep heather quickly becomes a problem. The steep slopes above Coire Fhar hold more snow and lead to a track in the coire. However to traverse these requires control on steep terrain and good judgement of the safety of the snow.

The descent from A' Mharconaich to Coire Dhomhain is steep and testing at the top, but easier in the lower reaches if there is snow that far down. It is best to return to the fence posts from the summit and follow S of these on a descending traverse to the track, which is then retraced to the start point.

If the route is skied in the other direction consideration must be given to crossing the Allt Coire Dhomhain on the return to the start point. It may be practical to aim for a higher crossing point, thus forsaking the superb running of a direct line back.

Alternatives

To the S of Sgairneach Mhor lies a snow-holding area of broad ridges, wide bowls and spacious glens. The slopes are easy. Snow lying in ribbons along the burns gives unexpected skiing when the surrounding moors are bare. To return to the start point of the main tour use can be made of the good track along the W side of Loch Garry to Dalnaspidal Lodge and the old road below the new A9, or if snow is lying high it may be preferable to return to the E flanks of Sgairneach Mhor and cross back over to Coire Dhomhain. Note however that the pass immediately W of the Sow of Atholl is threatened by avalanche-prone slopes.

"Garry Gully" is a good run following the valley of the Allt Coire Luidhearnaidh towards Dalnaspidal Lodge. It is considered by some to be the best run in the Drumochter area. There is one steep and restricted section towards the top of the turn, but it is otherwise quite easy. If snow runs out early there is a trudge across wet moor to Dalnaspidal Lodge or a climb back over to Coire Dhomhain. There is an excellent snow bowl immediately S of Sgairneach Mhor at the top of Coire na Garidha. A long run down this coire is often possible until late season, although it is then some distance back to the road. The valley of the Allt Coire Easan leads more conveniently to the track along Loch Garry. It also holds snow on easy slopes. It is easily reached from Sgairneach Mhor by traversing the SW flank of Meallan Buidhe. Further W the valley of the Allt na Glaise holds snow well in its upper reaches, but is even more remote from the road.

In bad weather shelter might be sought in Coire Dhomhain. It should be noted that steep slopes descend to this, which are prone to avalanche.

CORROUR AND RANNOCH STATIONS - THE WEST HIGHLAND RAILWAY LINE

From these two stations a vast area can be explored on skis along numerous routes, both at high and low levels. The absence of roads creates an atmosphere of remoteness, and the ability the skier has to glide freely over the snow-covered terrain permits passage across moorland exhausting to walk over in snow. The high level routes give exhilarating skiing but the low level routes also have a certain magic, for this is a beautiful and romantic area with a wild and awesome theme.

For those accustomed to skiing on tracks a circuit of Loch Ossian offers easy skiing. The tracks are good and snow is well preserved in the wooded areas, although the passage of vehicles can destroy the quality of the snow - thus the circuit is best skied just after snow fall. There are stunning views of shapely mountains, indeed Ben Nevis and mighty neighbours can be seen along the section from Corrour Station to the loch. At the time of writing a circuit can be achieved quite comfortably between train times, but if the allocated time is shortened take heart from those members of the "Run around Loch Ossian in Under One Hour Club" founded by Tom Rigg, warden of Loch Ossian Youth Hostel.

To the W of Corrour Station Coire a' Bhric Beag below Leum Uilleim holds the snow and gives sheltered skiing. An ascent of Leum Uilleim is well rewarded by views to the grand mountains of Glen Coe and the Blackmount beyond Rannoch Moor.

Beinn na Lap N of Loch Ossian can be skied from Corrour Station. It is a mountain of Munro status and a good viewpoint. Its slopes support an ideal base of short heather and grass, although there is a peppering of boulders too. The flanks are very steep and daunting but allow the competent to run long zig-zagging traverses across them in descent. If there is snow cover on the SW ridge (it may be blown clear) this gives the easiest angle for ascent.

Another route for those with mountain skills traverses Garbh-bheinn and Meall Garbh to the NE of Corrour Station. It descends to Fersit, from where a path leads E of the railway line for 2.5kms to Tulloch Station. There is a superb run down from Meall Garbh - see Tour 37.

If there is snow at low levels there are a number of routes following the glens which give fairly lengthy excursions through some grand mountain ranges and thrilling wild scenery. Fortunately there are tracks and paths along some of these, which aid running or if snow vanishes speed walking pace. These include routes N to Loch Treig and then on through Glen Nevis, Lairig Leacach or even to Kinlochleven via Loch Eilde Mor. Heading W from Rannoch Station it is possible to reach the Kingshouse Hotel and the A82 by venturing across Rannoch Moor. There is also the classic route E from Loch Ossian through the Ben Alder Range to Dalwhinnie. The mountains here are steep-sided and their ascents require advanced skiing techniques. However an easier route from Loch Ossian up the Uisge Labhair to the Bealach Dubh and the Allt a' Bhealaich Dhuibh gives more gentle skiing.

36. CARN DEARG AND SGOR GAIBHRE (THE RANNOCH FOREST HILLS)

OS SHEETS: 41 and 42   START POINT: Corrour Railway Station, GR 356664

TOTAL DISTANCE: 21kms   ASCENT: 785m   TIME: 6 hours 30 minutes

TERRAIN: Rich mix of easy Land-Rover tracks, open moorland, snow-filled burns and craggy mountain ridges.

SKIING ABILITIES REQUIRED: To ski whole route good ascent and descent skills and ability to cope with difficult snow conditions, however if prepared to walk some sections the less able will be able to ski some of the route.

OTHER ABILITIES REQUIRED: Excellent winter navigation and hillcraft skills.

SKIING EQUIPMENT NEEDED: Mountain touring gear.

OTHER EQUIPMENT NEEDED: Full mountain equipment.

SNOW COVER: Good. Tour starts at 400m above sea level and cover holds well on the N-facing slopes. Along part of the lochside the shade of the trees preserve the snow, however the quality of this may be destroyed by the passage of vehicles travelling between the station and the lodge. When snow is deficient in the lower sections the lochside track and the Road to the Isles give fast walking to snow at higher levels.

APPROACH ROADS: West Highland Railway Line to Corrour Station. Not served by public roads.

To ski this route requires planning, for train times must be checked, but also a degree of spontaneity, as it is best done when snow is lying on the lochside track, thus giving 7kms of wonderful track skiing in a beautiful mountain environment.

At the time of writing the rail service exists in an infrequent form. However an early morning train and an evening train allow sufficient time to complete this or other routes - except on a Sunday when there is only one train in each direction. There is no guarantee that this situation will improve. Loch Ossian Youth Hostel, GR 371671, is generally closed in winter although it is sometimes possible to arrange a special opening for groups. If so this makes an excellent

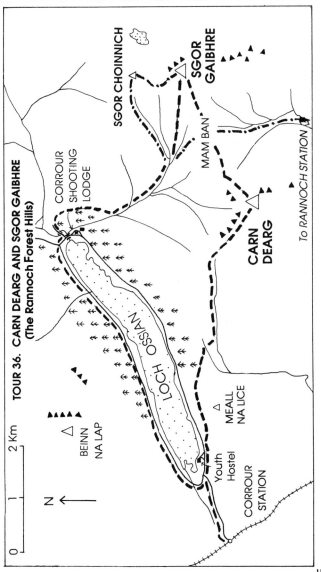

TOUR 36. CARN DEARG AND SGOR GAIBHRE
(The Rannoch Forest Hills)

base for ski touring in this area.

The route can be skied in either direction. The clockwise route is described here. Thus the majority of the track skiing is done first, and the most difficult section, the NE ridge of Carn Dearg, ascended rather than descended. The descent from Carn Dearg via the NW ridge and a tributary of the Allt a' Choire Odhair Bhig is a fine run towards magnificent scenery.

Follow the track heading E from the station to the old boathouse, now the youth hostel, at the W end of Loch Ossian. On a clear day, there are extensive views in all directions across a vast expanse of moorland. Of particular interest are Scotland's big mountains to the NW. There are views over the loch ahead too, with Beinn na Lap protecting its silvery peace from N winds.

The tracks on either side of the loch are skiable, but generally the N side is slightly better as the tree cover which preserves the snow is more extensive here and the track sandy and well-graded.

At the end of the loch a cluster of buildings constitute the present Corrour Shooting Lodge. The original lodge was destroyed by fire in 1942. It was a three-storey-high granite villa with a chapel, built by Sir John Maxwell of Glasgow. At one time it housed about fifty servants, gardeners and stalkers. Guests visiting this summer retreat were transported from Corrour Station to the pier where the youth hostel now stands, and then taken by a small steamer across the loch. Indeed there were plans to build a canal between the loch and the railway so that guests need not be subjected to the rough ride along the track. Only a handful of people now live here and a bungalow marks the site of the original lodge at the NE corner of the loch. A fire engine is kept parked ready to fight any repeat fires and to satisfy the insurance companies.

The route ascends from the loch up the wide valley of the Allt a' Choire Chreagaich. Access to this is barred by trees, and although there are routes through them, these are often wet, bouldery and strewn with fallen trees. From the track on the N side of the loch it is better to bear NE just before the bridge over the River Ossian, to cross this 100m downstream by another bridge, thus following the good track heading into the valley of the Uisge Labhair. Beyond a stance of trees leave this path and head S across the moor to skirt woods and thus gain the route up the Allt a' Choire Chreagaich. This is a very easy angled ascent of a grass and heathery base where the snow lingers in ribbons after thaw elsewhere. The upper bowl stretching from the col Mam Ban around to Meall Nathrach Mor is a good skiing area with some fine descents and practice areas. Of particular note are the snow-holding NW-facing flank of Sgor Gaibhre, (which is quite steep but plenty broad), and the descents from Bealach nan Sgor and Sgor Choinnich W down tributaries of the Allt a' Choire Chreagaich.

The route ascends the NW flank of Sgor Gaibhre to the summit cairn, however it is possible to include an ascent of Sgor Choinnich first. This involves skiing on some steep but broad ground. From both these summits there are views to the elusive Ben Alder and across Loch Ericht. There are also steep and nasty slopes falling away to the E - quite a contrast to the ski slopes ascended on the W side.

Descend the broad SW ridge of Sgor Gaibhre to the flat and often draughty col of Mam Ban. Immediately to the N and S are easy practice runs, and it is possible to ski from here on gentle slopes down Coire Eigheach and the valley of the Allt Eigheach to Rannoch Station. This route is only worthwhile if there is complete snow cover at low levels. If this is the case and weather or ability limits desire to climb the peaks, a pleasant Nordic outing linking Corrour and Rannoch stations can be made via Mam Ban (wind direction determining direction skied).

From Mam Ban the route ascends the NE ridge of Carn Dearg. Although easy above the col, this steepens near the summit and gives a short section of restricted skiing prone to icing. It is not a major problem in ascent if skins are used, but if descended requires controlled skiing. Some will prefer to walk it in descent.

From the summit cairn of Carn Dearg turn NW and follow the ridge for 1km. On a clear day views of Ben Nevis and the Mamores lie ahead. Gain the open snow bowl of a tributary of the Allt a' Choire Odhair Bhig, which gives a pleasant descent W to the good track "The Road to the Isles". This leads back to the youth hostel and the Land-Rover track to Corrour Station.

37. CHNO DEARG

OS SHEET: 41

START POINT: End of public road at Fersit, GR 351782

TOTAL DISTANCE: 13kms   ASCENT: 857m   TIME: 4 hours 45 minutes

TERRAIN: Easy angled mountain slopes. Rounded bouldery summits.

SKIING ABILITIES REQUIRED: Basic skills of ascent and descent.

OTHER ABILITIES REQUIRED: Excellent winter navigation and hillcraft skills.

SKIING EQUIPMENT NEEDED: General or mountain touring gear.

OTHER EQUIPMENT NEEDED: Full mountain equipment.

SNOW COVER: Classic N-facing burns hold snow well. Westerly location means generally has less snow, and faster thaw than routes further E. Can be checked from the A86.

APPROACH ROADS: A86 Glen Spean, then minor road W of Tulloch Station to Fersit.

The N-facing, long and gentle slopes leading to this accessible Munro Summit make Chno Dearg a classic mountain for Nordic touring. This is a short and uncomplicated mountain tour to fine viewpoints and with a long uninterrupted running descent.

Cross the River Treig and the West Highland Railway and follow the minor road E to the end of the hamlet. Turn S onto the open moor by sheep pens and a barn. Ascend easily the slopes drained by the Allt Chaorach Beag, to the superfluously named Lochan Coire an Lochain, nestling below the mighty buttresses of Stob Coire Sgriodain. The area hereabouts is a good practice area well sheltered from westerly winds. Continue SE without difficult to the broad col GR 368735. In clear conditions it is inspiring to see Buachaille Etive Mor 24kms SW from this col.

It is possible to ski Stob Coire Sgriodain from the col. However this lies 2kms away, over two minor summits, and the going is difficult over rocky, bouldery terrain prone to being blown clear (approximately 1.5 hours return to the col). Meall Garbh on the other hand can

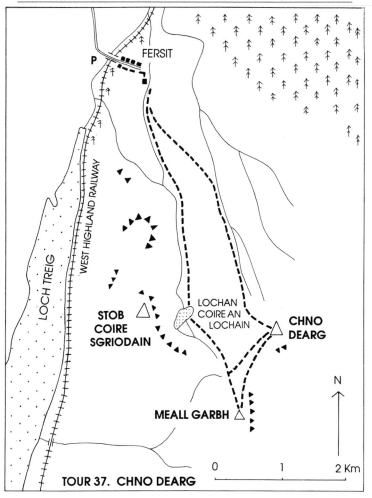

FERSIT

P

CHNO DEARG

STOB COIRE SGRIODAIN

LOCHAN COIRE AN LOCHAIN

MEALL GARBH

LOCH TREIG

WEST HIGHLAND RAILWAY

N

0   1   2 Km

TOUR 37. CHNO DEARG

161

easily be added, within as little as 30 minutes return to the col. The gentle rise from the col up the broad N ridge gives an easy ascent rewarded generously by extensive views S from the cairn on the S Top. Note the E flank of Meall Garbh falls away to steep crags.

From the col ascend steadily NE to reach the flat summit of Chno Dearg. This is boulder-strewn and may be blown clear. It is a fine viewpoint. Creag Meagaidh and neighbouring hills justify the N, Rannoch Moor sprawls S with the hills of Glen Coe and the Black Mount beyond. Close by Stob Coire Sgriodain rears to the W.

The descent to Fersit is steepest in the upper section, but broad flanks and unrestricting terrain minimise difficulties. It is possible to take a direct line, or descend to the SW col (GR 372735) and then turn NNW to traverse the slopes E of and above Lochan Coire an Lochain. The course of the burns across the lower moor give the best snow and easiest running.

38. RANNOCH FOREST

OS SHEET: 42 OR 51

START POINT: Picnic Place and Car Park at Carie, GR 617572

TOTAL DISTANCE: 9kms   ASCENT: 170m   TIME: 2 hours 30 minutes

TERRAIN: Easy forest roads and paths.

SKIING ABILITIES REQUIRED: Most of tour is easy. One short section of restricted skiing can be walked.

OTHER ABILITIES REQUIRED: Elementary map reading skills.

SKIING EQUIPMENT NEEDED: Light touring gear.

OTHER EQUIPMENT NEEDED: Lightweight equipment.

SNOW COVER: Dependent on snow lying at low levels, tour lies between 230m and 400m above sea level. Short season, confined to the winter months.

APPROACH ROADS: Minor road along S side of Loch Rannoch from Kinloch Rannoch. Parking at start point.

Rannoch Forest lies away from the main centres of population and

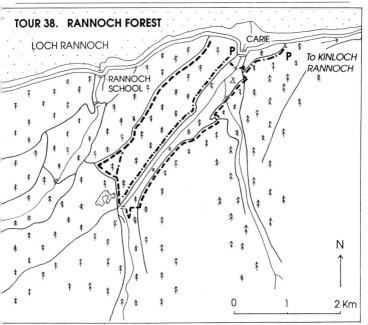

TOUR 38. RANNOCH FOREST

LOCH RANNOCH

CARIE

RANNOCH SCHOOL

To KINLOCH RANNOCH

N

0   1   2 Km

traditional skiing grounds, and so is often scorned in favour of nearer or better known venues. However it is well worth a visit for there are many kilometres of peaceful skiing on sound forest track here. Views over the surrounding moor open out above the tall trees and although this is commercial plantation, there is a lacing of fine spreading Scots pines, and idyllic stances of birches. A N-facing aspect and the shade of the trees assist snow-holding.

The chosen route is a short and easy introduction to the forest. The many extensions and alternatives are clearly shown on the relevant 1:50,000 OS map, with the route to Glen Lyon via Lairig Ghallabhaich an attractive option.

The route starts at the picnic place and car park just W of the bridge over the Carie Burn, but can also be accessed from the car park E of Carie at GR 626573.

Cross the Carie Burn by the footbridge by the toilets at the car park. The burn is funnelled between slab and gorge here, and then flows

Delightful skiing in Rannoch Forest. Picnic place and footbridge over the Allt na Bogair

via the alluvial fan of its own creation into Loch Rannoch. A path leads quickly to a broad forest track, which is then followed S along the perimeter of the campsite to a junction of paths and the route from the other car park. The track straight ahead has a boom across it. Go up this turning right almost immediately, onto another broad track. After 1km continue SW at a junction, passing through a deer fence. Follow for 2kms above the steep S bank of the Allt na Bogair. The route then descends a narrow gap in the trees where a summer path leads down to the burn. This gap is marked by a waymarker post, just after the viewpoint shown on some OS maps and a bench above the track. The descent requires a repertoire of techniques which may include walking. In addition to the obvious difficulties of skiing down a narrow gap through trees there are drainage ditches, an old wire fence and steep banks to negotiate. However the difficulties are short-lived and the gradient never steep for long. It is of course practical to ski this tour in the opposite direction and ascend this section thus eliminating difficulty, but also the fun and excitement of a good forest trail. The track weaves down to meet the burn at a bridge and picnic spot.

It is possible to ski directly back from here to the start point along a good track following the N bank of the Allt na Bogair. For a longer tour continue N, past a walled loch, for 1km to a junction with a forest road leading NE. This descends gradually to meet the road 0.5km W of the start point. A path links these two tracks and dissects the corner. However it is not a worthwhile short cut. The first part is very pleasant, but lower down the way is bouldery and adopted by the course of a stream, which if not frozen gives wet and hopeless skiing.

39. TUMMEL FOREST

OS SHEET: 43   START POINT: Car park and picnic place, GR 857601
TOTAL DISTANCE: 9.5kms   ASCENT: 200m   TIME: 2 hours 45 minutes
TERRAIN: Road, track and trail through thick mature forest. Gradients mostly easy.
SKIING ABILITIES REQUIRED: Suit beginner who may walk some sections.
OTHER ABILITIES REQUIRED: Basic winter navigation skills
SKIING EQUIPMENT NEEDED: Light touring gear.
OTHER EQUIPMENT NEEDED: Lightweight equipment.
SNOW COVER: Dependent on snow lying at 250m. Best chances in January and February.
APPROACH ROADS: B8019 Killiecrankie to Tummel Bridge.

If you think forest skiing is boring and monotonous, try this one! There is more here than unchallenging forest roads imprisoned in tall conifer walls. This is a good place for family skiing.

The route described has been chosen because it gives varied skiing to points of interest. However there are many other tracks and trails here, including the waymarked nature trail circuits. The tour itself can be extended, or skied in either direction.

A note of caution: some forest roads and tracks are not marked on the OS maps exactly as they occur on the ground, some are not marked at all, and frequently the way through is not immediately obvious or ignored for a more promising looking opening in the trees. In any event the workings of the Forestry Commission may completely change the appearance of an area, and felling can render

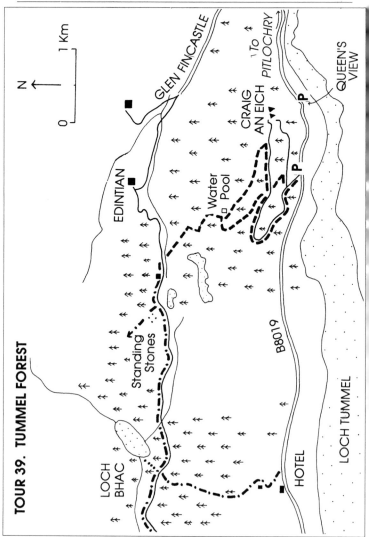

TOUR 39. TUMMEL FOREST

areas impassable on skis. The 1:25,000 scale map is useful and it is recommendable to carry a compass.

From the car park ascend NW the broad forest road. A road joining from the right carries the eventual route of return. Continue uphill to reach a renovated clachan. The route ascends steadily until a broad sweeping turn to the right leads to level skiing. To return this way to the car park gives a pleasant downhill run. The route this far is along the red (Clachan), blue (Allean), and yellow (Clunie) waymarked trails. The red route now departs to the right, to return to the start point. Thirty yards beyond a trail leads up the N bank. Leave the waymarked road, and follow this unmarked rather bumpy trail uphill, direction NW, for approximately 1km. Continue until the trail bends sharply right to meet a broad track by a fenced pool of water. There is an old light blue and white marker post here, and at the time of writing some decrepit fire fighting brushes.

Turn left and ski easily for 0.5km passing through a gap in a broken-down wall. Watch out for the track leading NW, marked in the past by a blue and white marker, (which may or may not be still standing). Follow this track to meet a forest road. Turn left, and so reach the route from Edintian. Just W of this junction there is a small wooden shed above the track. It is in good repair, and furnished with simple benches.

From this bothy it is only a short and very pleasant ski to visit the standing stones at GR 838620. A trail leaves the forest road by the bend and small turning area just E of Lochan na Leathain. There are four stumps on the W of the track, arranged in a circle and showing the four points of the compass. The trail continues past them and if followed gives delightful explorative skiing.

The tour can be extended to Loch Bhac. This is a very easy ski along the sound based forest road. Loch Bhac is signposted at the junction, GR 818619, however from here the track leads directly to the loch, not as shown on some OS maps. It has a dubious rubble and stone base, ideal for wrecking ski soles. The loch is a beautiful place, worth visiting. It is possible to ski from the junction to rejoin the B8019 by the hotel at Tressait, along an easy ride which leaves the forest road opposite the Loch Bhac track.

If returning from the bothy to the start point an alternative to the outward route continues straight on (SE) at the fenced-in water pool (GR 853610). The track is followed for 1km to rejoin the forest road and the waymarked nature trails. It is joined en route by various rides and a new forest road. There is a choice of routes to return by. The yellow trail goes to Craig an Eich, but the most direct way back to the start point is to ski W along the forest road to join the outward route and then follow the red route narrowly down to the lower forest road, which is skied W to rejoin the outward route just above the car park.

40. THE BLACK MOUNT

OS SHEET: 50   START POINT: Forest Lodge, GR 270423

TOTAL DISTANCE: 14kms   ASCENT: 230m   TIME: 4 hours

TERRAIN: Good Land-Rover track (9kms) and open moor. Gentle slopes.

SKIING ABILITIES REQUIRED: Mostly easy skiing but some ascent and descent requiring basic snowplough ability.

OTHER ABILITIES REQUIRED: Basic winter navigation skills

SKIING EQUIPMENT NEEDED: General touring gear. Light gear if skiing on track only, or if snow conditions are suitable.

OTHER EQUIPMENT NEEDED: Light rucksack.

SNOW COVER: Unreliable. Some winters allow no skiing on the Black Mount at all. Low start point for this route (170m). In lean conditions it may be preferable to ski from the A82 at Loch Ba, which is higher (300m).

APPROACH ROADS: A82 to Bridge of Orchy, then A8005 to Victoria Bridge.

Skiing on the Black Mount is for opportunists. Snow comes and goes quickly. The area lies at a height below that of the car park at the White Corries skiing development - and downhill skiers who frequent the lifts there will appreciate how often (or not) snow lies thereabouts. However, if there is snow, the Black Mount is a good place to ski. It is surrounded by imposing mountains, but the basin itself is ideal gentle terrain. In summer the moor is wet, desolate and unattractive to walkers. In winter the shallow lochans freeze and exploration on ski is effortless.

The A82 crosses the Black Mount, climbing above 300m, and giving

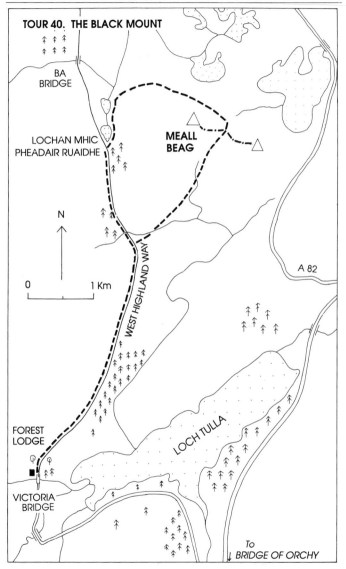

TOUR 40. THE BLACK MOUNT

BA BRIDGE

LOCHAN MHIC PHEADAIR RUAIDHE

MEALL BEAG

N

0   1 Km

WEST HIGHLAND WAY

A 82

LOCH TULLA

FOREST LODGE

VICTORIA BRIDGE

To
BRIDGE OF ORCHY

easy access to any snow there might be. This is a major trunk road kept open except in extreme conditions. A path crosses from the A82 to the ruined Ba Cottage and is a good route into the area. This leaves the A82 at GR 308497, at 300m above sea level. The West Highland Way also crosses the Black Mount, and if snow is low-lying this is probably the choice route to take, for it gives excellent track skiing to Ba Cottage, passes through varied wood and moorland scenery, and offers exceptional views of the Black Mount peaks and across Loch Tulla to the mountain beasts E of the West Highland Railway Line. The route described here follows the Way and then heads across the moor to give a pleasantly varied ski tour.

From Forest Lodge follow the West Highland Way for 5.5kms to Lochan Mhic Pheadair Ruaidhe. The Way follows the old Glen Coe Road. This is a metalled road giving a consistent and mostly boulder-free base to the snow. It ascends steadily, and it will probably be necessary to walk to the snow line. The lochan may be frozen and skiable. It provides a good practice area for beginners, with the flat expanse of the lochan complementing low hillocks with slopes of varying angles and safe run-outs.

From the lochan ski downstream (N), but before reaching the River Ba head E to skirt the N flank of Meall Beag. Taking care not to gain too much height maintain a slightly rising traverse across the lower slopes to gain the easy route leading S to the col between Meall Beag and its higher neighbour to the SE. Both summits are skiable from the col. The snow cover on these two hills can be checked from the A82 to both S and N. They are worth visiting for the extensive view across Rannoch Moor and the Black Mount to giant mountains beyond.

From the col descend broad easy slopes SW to reach the West Highland Way once again and return via the outward route to Forest Lodge.

41. BEINN ACHALADAIR AND BEINN A' CHREACHAIN

OS SHEET: 50   START POINT: Achallader Farmhouse, GR 320443

TOTAL DISTANCE: 18kms   ASCENT: 1,233m   TIME: 6 hours 30 minutes

TERRAIN: Mountain slopes of all gradients. One narrow arête.

SKIING ABILITIES REQUIRED: Ability to climb, traverse and descend steep slopes and move over ice and mixed rock and ice. Expert skills and control needed if the arête is skied, but this can be walked.

OTHER ABILITIES REQUIRED: Excellent winter navigation and hillcraft skills. High level of fitness.

SKIING EQUIPMENT NEEDED: Mountain touring gear.

OTHER EQUIPMENT NEEDED: Full mountain equipment.

SNOW COVER: Despite high altitude and good aspect snow cover is unreliable. Snow line in Coire Achaladair can be seen from A82 N of Loch Tulla.

APPROACH ROADS: A82 Bridge of Orchy to Glen Coe. 1km S of the bridge over the Water of Tulla a private, rough track leads to Achallader Farmhouse.

This is one of the finest ski tours in Scotland. Beinn Achaladair and Beinn a' Chreachain are star performers in the Munro plot. Their bold characters appear to motorists on the A82 on the descent from Rannoch Moor to Loch Tulla, from where the snow cover of some of the route can be studied. The tour includes several kilometres when the skier is kept high to enjoy gallery views of the surrounding mountains, the Black Mount and Rannoch Moor. The skiing at times is advanced and demanding, but if the less-able are willing to walk sections there is some skiing on offer here for them too.

From Achallader Farm a track leads S to a footbridge over the West Highland Railway. The route ascends steadily and easily up Coire Achaladair to the col between Beinn an Dothaidh and Beinn Achaladair. From here turn N to climb the easy angled, but often icy and windblown slope of the S ridge and so gain the South Top.

A broad and easily skied ridge joins the South Top with the main

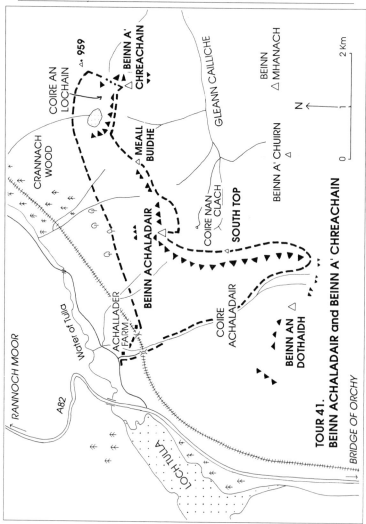

TOUR 41.
BEINN ACHALADAIR and BEINN A' CHREACHAIN

summit to the N. Beware, in poor visibility of the cliffs immediately to the W and N of the route, and in particular take care at the summit, beyond which the land drops away dramatically. In clear conditions this is a viewpoint of magnitude.

From the summit the descent leads to the col at GR 353435. If skied directly it leads into steep rock and boulder-strewn terrain above the col. This can be avoided by skiing S into the easier snow bowl of Coire nan Clach and then descending E and then NE to the col, carefully choosing a route to avoid the rocks or descending too far below the col.

From the col 170m of steady but straightforward ascent brings you to the broad summit ridge of Meall Buidhe. Follow this to its NE end, perched high above the imposing cliffs of Coire an Lochain, and skirt these travelling E and then up steeply to the high point and summit cairn of Beinn a' Chreachain.

Closely watching map and compass in mist gain the NE ridge. This is very narrow, likely to be corniced, and quite impossible for many skiers, who will wish to cautiously walk it. However it has been skied on Nordic mountain touring skis. The difficulties/walking are short-lived and the ridge widens giving a classy and easy run-out to the col just before point 959m. The slopes descending into Coire an Lochain are steep, but a grassy base and broad area for traverses and kick turns allow the less-able to descend comfortably. Cross the floor of the coire below the flat frozen lochan and head WSW for home on an easy, but lengthy, slowly descending traverse above Crannach Wood through scattered birch trees and over a series of snow-filled burns. Calculate your route carefully so that the traverse brings you after approximately 4kms to the railway line by the house and footbridge above Achallader Farm, thus maximising use of gravity.

42. BEINN MHANACH

OS SHEET: 50   START POINT: A82. Road to Auch Farm.

TOTAL DISTANCE: 21kms   ASCENT: 738m   TIME: 6 hours 30 minutes

TERRAIN: Broad track leading to grassy slopes. Mostly easy angled, but steepening in places.

SKIING ABILITIES REQUIRED: Ability to climb, traverse and descend broad hillside and cope with varied snow conditions.

OTHER ABILITIES REQUIRED: Good winter navigation and hillcraft skills. General fitness.

SKIING EQUIPMENT NEEDED: Mountain touring gear.

OTHER EQUIPMENT NEEDED: Full mountain equipment.

SNOW COVER: Unfortunately opportunities to ski the whole of this route are rare. The westerly location, low level of the first part of the route, lack of forest and the sunny aspect means snow comes and goes quickly. However if the route is in condition this is a superb Nordic ski tour.

APPROACH ROADS: A82 between Tyndrum and Bridge of Orchy. Note: minor road to Auch Farm is a private road.

Not in the traditional high level plateau Nordic ski touring zones, yet when in condition this mountain tour ranks with some of the best in Scotland. The long, easy angled approach is well suited to an ascent on Nordic mountain touring skis. There is relaxed skiing along riverside track, a challenging steady climb and a running descent. The scenery in inspiring.

From the A82 descend the private road to the bridge beyond Auch Farm. Keeping SE of the Allt Kinglass (Allt Chonoghlais) head NE up Auch Gleann. A track leads up the glen, reaching a height of 550m W of Beinn a' Chuirn. This gives the langlauf skier a hefty advantage for his launch up the mountain, marred only by the numerous times the track fords the Allt Kinglass before Ais-an t-Sidhean. If crossing the river is not easy stay on the SE bank. From the sheep pens at Ais-an t-Sidhean temporarily leave the track as it detours E, and ascend due N up easy grass-based slopes to regain the track further uphill. This

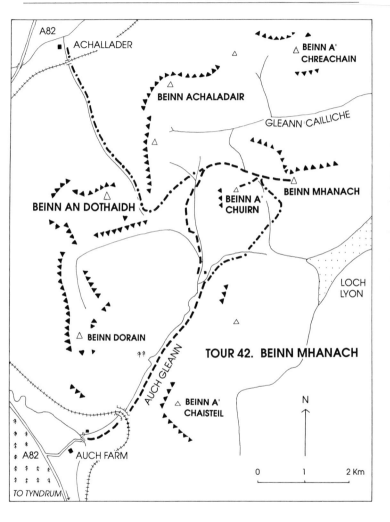

is then ascended until it terminates (or disappears under the snow). Just before reaching the fence posts and the col at GR 354418 leave the burn and ascend E around the steepening slopes of Beinn a' Chuirn to the col separating Beinn Mhanach from Beinn a' Chuirn. The fence posts lead from the lower to the upper col. A gate at the upper col is a useful marker in mist.

Inclusion of Beinn a' Chuirn adds 20 minutes to the journey. It is best approached on skis from the col, as the slope here is kind, unlike the steep and craggy slopes guarding the other flanks.

From the col Beinn Mhanach lies 1km of steady ascent to the E. The view from the summit reveals mountains in all directions, and in particular their potential for ski tours. Certainly the Bridge of Orchy giants, which look frighteningly steep from the A82, show their back doors offering more scope to skiers.

To return via the outward route is straightforward and probably gives the best snow and most enjoyable ski run. However for those who prefer steeper gradients it is possible to descend the steep S-facing slope down to the Allt a' Chuirn when snow cover is good. Note that this S-facing slope is prone to icing and what looked like a super run from the valley below can be hard in both meanings of the word. Although long easy angled traverses can be linked by kick turns on a broad flank, all but downhill devils will probably benefit most from going the other way! Mind you, the route along the Allt a' Chuirn has fascinating snow-holding secrets.

It is also possible, and recommended if transport can be arranged, to return to Achallader Farm via the Allt Coire Achaladair. This involves returning NW to the col at GR 354418 and traversing to the col between Beinn an Dothaidh and Beinn Achaladair. There is 140m of ascent, and the slope to be traversed is steep, but this route has advantages when the snow line is high as all but the last kilometre lie above the 300m contour line. (The last 6kms of the main route are below 300m.) Indeed in poor snow conditions this N-facing valley may be preferable in ascent too. (See Tour 41 for description of ascent from Achallader Farm to col between Beinn an Dothaidh and Beinn Achaladair.)

43. MEALL BUIDHE, GLEANN DAIMH

OS SHEET: 51

START POINT: End of road by dam, Loch an Daimh, GR 509463

TOTAL DISTANCE: 15kms   ASCENT: 730m   TIME: 5 hours

TERRAIN: Grassy undulating hills rising to high point at Meall Buidhe. 3kms of loch-side track on return. Generally easy slopes at upper levels although some steep sections to reach them.

SKIING ABILITIES REQUIRED: Ability to ascend and descend short, steep but broad slopes and cope with difficult snow conditions if including Meall Buidhe. The upland area W of Meall Buidhe is easy terrain, and once reached requires basic skills only.

OTHER ABILITIES REQUIRED: Excellent winter navigation and hillcraft skills.

SKIING EQUIPMENT NEEDED: Mountain touring gear.

OTHER EQUIPMENT NEEDED: Full mountain equipment.

SNOW COVER: Some excellent N-facing snow-holding slopes, reached by poorer cover on S-facing slopes. However, grassy nature of the hills and ability to drive to 400m above sea level and ascend easily means skiable snow can be reached quickly.

APPROACH ROADS: Minor road up Glen Lyon. Turn right 2kms W of Meggernie Castle to ascend minor road to the dam of Loch an Daimh. Parking below the dam. Road may well be impassable after snowfall. Note also the minor road from Loch Tay to Bridge of Balgie is frequently blocked during the winter - even when the weather at Loch Tay or in Glen Lyon seems tame and spring-like.

N of Loch an Daimh, between Glen Lyon and Rannoch Moor lies an area of grassy upland of easy undulating Nordic touring terrain. It is quickly reached by a short stiff climb up steep grassy slopes above the loch. The high point is Meall Buidhe, a mountain of Munro status, and well situated above the expanse of Rannoch Moor to view Scotland's central mountain ranges. This is an area where good Nordic downhill running and ski-exploring can be enjoyed.

From the dam ascend N up initially steep slopes on a short grass base to the bowl of Coire nam Miseach below Meall a' Phuill. Ascend

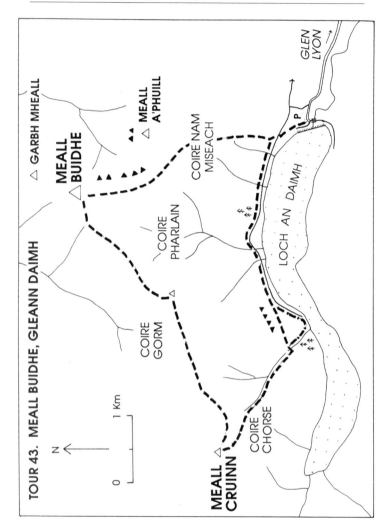

TOUR 43. MEALL BUIDHE, GLEANN DAIMH

NW to the southerly point of the long, curved summit ridge, which is then followed for 1km to the summit cairn of Meall Buidhe. On a clear day more and more mountains come into view throughout the ascent culminating in the panorama of peaks which can be identified from the summit. The long summit ridge is prone to blowing clear, leaving an unskiable rocky base along the top and large cornices grinning down the steep E face. Thus the W flank provides a safer and more pleasant ascent. From the summit ridge the terrain and snow cover to the W can be studied and the onward route chosen. The NW-facing flank above the upper reaches of the Allt Sloc na Creadha appears particularly worthwhile.

From the summit of Meall Buidhe there is a fine descent SW to the col at GR 487491, initially down the snow bowl above the tributary of the Allt Sloc na Creadha, and then on the NW-facing flanks of the broad cairned ridge trending WSW from the summit. From the col it is worth ascending to the cairn on the high point, GR 482485, as there is an easy and enjoyable run from here W to the flat col E of Meall Cruinn.

Meall Cruinn is more rocky than its neighbours, but can easily be ascended up snow-holding ribbons leading to the summit. There is further exploration W or NE from Meall Cruinn, however it is also a good place to start the return from, as easy slopes lead down the S ridge (old fence posts) and into Coire Chorse. Lower down the burn has incised deeply, but there is a good descent on the flanks W of it, where snow collects in patches and ribbons.

When snow cover is good it is possible from about a height of 550m to descend gradually E to the loch-side track, by traversing grassy slopes above the loch, keeping below the crags above this height. If snow cover does not permit this the loch-side track provides easy walking back to the dam with fine views into the Coire of Stuchd an Lochain and ahead to Ben Lawers. This track has been extended 1km beyond the point indicated on the current OS map, and reaches to just E of the burn of descent.

44. THE CARN MAIRG GROUP, GLEN LYON

OS SHEET: 51   START POINT: Invervar, GR 666482

TOTAL DISTANCE: 15.5kms   ASCENT: 1,200m   TIME: 6 hours

TERRAIN: Broad open hillside leading to long and wide high level ridge connecting flat-topped Munro Summits. Descent down snow-filled corrie and burn. Slopes most easy angled, but some steeper sections.

SKIING ABILITIES REQUIRED: Competent ascent and descent skills. Ability to cope with difficult ice/snow conditions.

OTHER ABILITIES REQUIRED: Good winter navigation skills.

SKIING EQUIPMENT NEEDED: Mountain touring gear.

OTHER EQUIPMENT NEEDED: Full mountain equipment.

SNOW COVER: Crest of main ridge generally blown clear exposing unskiable stony ground. Some good snow-holding on grassy flanks lower down. Snow holds particularly well in Coire Chearcaille and S and E of the Allt Coire a' Chearcaill. Elevated height means usually some skiing until April.

APPROACH ROADS: Minor road in Glen Lyon to Invervar.

It is unfortunate that these hills do not hold snow well along the main high level traverse, for this is an otherwise excellent circuit for Nordic tourers across ideal spacious terrain and with extensive inspiring views of the high mountains of Central Scotland.

The route links three Munro Summits, with little loss of height between tops, and passes within easy skiing of a fourth summit of Munro status. Further good Nordic routes allow extensions to or shorter variations of the circuit described.

From the telephone kiosk at Invervar take the track leading N along the E bank of Invervar Burn. Cross the burn at the tree-line and ascend W the easy snow-holding NE-facing slopes. Turn NW up steeper slopes to approach the summit of Carn Gorm.

Descend the broad but steep-sided N ridge, and traverse the snow-holding NW flank of An Sgorr to reach Meall Garbh. The terrain becomes more stony and windswept along the route E to Carn Mairg, and the skier may well be forced away from the broad crest to seek

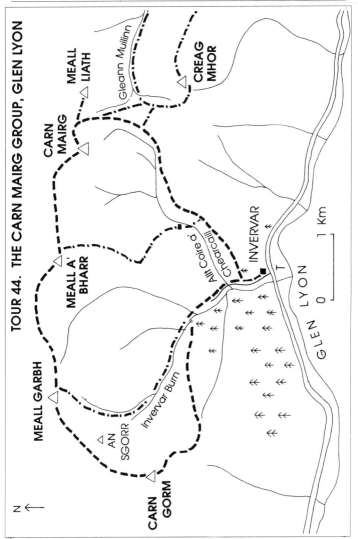

TOUR 44. THE CARN MAIRG GROUP, GLEN LYON

snow in the corries and flanks below the ridge. If snow cover is intact this is a classic Nordic high level traverse commanding excellent views in all directions. A line of dilapidated fence posts along this section greatly assists navigation in mist but otherwise inconveniently litters the route.

From Carn Mairg the route returns to Invervar along the renowned ski descent of the Allt Coire a' Chearcaill. This is a snow-holding run down open easy slopes. Carn Mairg is flanked by steep slopes to the SW and boulders to the E. It is preferable to keep N of the boulder fields and descend to the col before Meall Liath and then S to begin the descent. There is a bothy at GR 673497 from which a track, useful if snow cover has expired, descends to the outward route just N of Invervar.

Alternatives

1. The fourth Munro Summit of the area, Creag Mhor lies only 2kms of high level skiing from the summit of Carn Mairg. The terrain is easy and snow holds on the grass and moss summit plateau and N-facing slope of the mountain. It is still the best option, if including this ascent, to retrace steps N across the superb N flank and return to Invervar via the classic descent of the Allt Coire a' Chearcaill. However there are fine routes to Fortingall along the SE ridge of the mountain or via Gleann Muilinn.

2. A shorter circuit, utilising mostly broad and uncomplicated slopes ascends the Invervar Burn to Meall Garbh, returning via the broad ridge of Meall a' Bharr to the Allt Coire a' Chearcaill. The corrie between Meall a' Bharr and Carn Mairg has a steep but skiable headwall and the snow holds well in the long run-out along the burn to the bothy.

45. THE BEN LAWERS AREA

OS SHEET: 51

Ben Lawers, its surrounding mountains, corries and moorland offers enormous scope for the Nordic skier, with terrain suitable for all abilities from the absolute beginner to the hunter of extreme steep slopes.

One of the main reasons for the popularity of this area is the minor road from the A827 to Bridge of Balgie. This climbs to a height of 550m and provides quick access to the height where snow might be expected. It is a good bet if you don't want to walk too far.

For the beginner there are some excellent nursery areas, for the mountain tourer, classic high level traverses. But the track skiing is inferior, and the mountain environment open house to the Scottish winter weather.

1. The Road to Bridge of Balgie

This is not cleared of snow, but usually there is sufficient passage of traffic to the National Trust for Scotland Visitor Centre to keep the road passable by vehicles to this point in winter (height 430m). However it should be noted that there is a steep, and often icy hill close to the junction with the A827 and a narrow bridge just below the Visitor Centre, where cars are known to have come a cropper in snowy conditions. Snow chains are sometimes required on this road. The Visitor Centre is closed in winter.

The road gives an even base for skiing. The section along Lochan na Lairige is often snow-covered giving good skiing in rugged surroundings. There is easy skiing on the road immediately N of the Visitor Centre and crossing the moor E of the Burn of Edramucky. The section through the forest above the A827, however, is steep and restricted. The S-facing aspect means this section is affected by the sun, and at this lower altitude, freeze-thaw and ice formation are common.

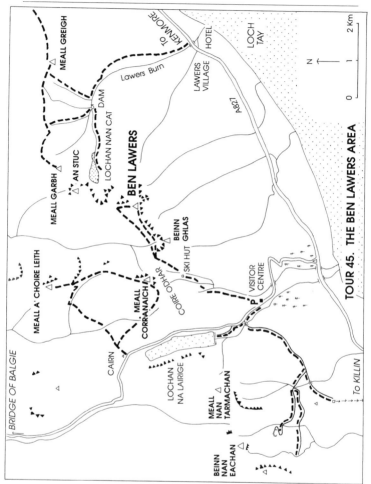

TOUR 45. THE BEN LAWERS AREA

2. Area below the Dam

The area immediately S of the huge dam of Lochan na Lairige is well suited for beginners' needs. It offers some shelter in an otherwise weather-beaten area. It is easily approached via a level track branching from the road. The terrain is grassy and the slopes kind.

3. Tracks to the W of the Road

Midway between the Visitor Centre and the dam a track leads W from the road. It branches after 3kms. One branch descends S of Meall Liath to an edifice from which penstocks descend to a small power station on Loch Tay. The other branch divides after 0.5km, one spur climbing to a disused quarry and ruined building, the other leading W across open moor. These tracks offer very easy mind-numbing skiing. The only problem is rapid thaw on sun-facing slopes, and the only interest the view across Loch Tay, or in the case of the upper track, of the Tarmachan Hills. However they are popular with novices attracted to the Ben Lawers nursery slopes, for whom their gradients cause some degree of panic and prayers, but which should be quite within the capabilities of those who have mastered elementary techniques. It is possible to link the tracks by skiing over the intervening moor.

4. Coire Odhar

In days gone by this coire was one of the major centres of Scottish skiing. Activity was based around the hut belonging to the Scottish Ski Club, erected in 1932. The hut (locked) is still there today (GR 616401), although the coire is quiet now, and the races, events and happy skisters part of the past. Even the modern day hordes dashing up Ben Lawers do not go into the coire, but follow the Tourist Path up the SW ridge of Beinn Ghlas. The coire therefore welcomes the Nordic skier who appreciates the untrodden snow fields, sheltered as they are by high mountains.

The coire lies NNE of the Visitor Centre, the ski hut being approximately one hour's skiing from the car park. The ascent is steep in places, and the descent requires downhill skiing ability (snow plough at very least), but the schuss down the coire from the col between Meall Corranaich and Beinn Ghlas is worth the effort of the ascent. In poor visibility it may be difficult to find the ski hut. The coire floor N of the hut has good learning terrain for novices, whilst the sides are steeper and suitable for more advanced practice. Ribbons of snow extending along the burns give some good corridor skiing after thaw on the surrounding moor.

5. Ben Lawers

Ben Lawers is renowned as a skier's mountain. Sadly it is not within the capabilities of many Nordic skiers, although it is skiable on mountain Nordic touring gear. The slopes are steep, exposed and frequently icy, the skiing is restricted and demands complete control on narrow ridges. It is more suited to ski mountaineering gear, which is better designed to deal with steep gradients and hard ice.

The popular ascent from the Visitor Centre is via the Tourist Path over Beinn Ghlas. However on Nordic skis it is more practical to ascend Coire Odhar to the col between Beinn Ghlas and Meall Corranaich from where the route bypasses Beinn Ghlas and ascends E on a rising traverse across the NW-facing slopes of Beinn Ghlas to the col between Beinn Ghlas and Ben Lawers. The final ascent up the SW ridge is awkward, being steep and rocky, with the NW flank of the ridge giving the better option. The descent can follow the route of ascent, or continue N to the col between Ben Lawers and An Stuc before turning SW to return to the col at the head of Coire Odhar across natural shelves in the NW-facing slopes of Ben Lawers and Beinn Ghlas.

6. Meall Corranaich and Meall a' Choire Leith

These two mountains of Munro status lie W of Ben Lawers, and can both be skied on mountain touring gear in a day's outing. To ski the whole route one must be competent on steep slopes. However there is much easy going too, and skiers with basic touring skills, prepared to walk difficult sections, will still find the tour worthwhile.

Meall Corranaich can be ascended from the Visitor Centre via the S ridge, but the best way is from the cairn at the high point on the road, just N of Lochan na Lairige. The route ascends SE across easy slopes to the course of the Allt Gleann Da-Eig, continuing up the coire to the S ridge, which is then followed to the summit plateau. In order to avoid difficulties keep to the W flanks as the summit is approached, and walk if in doubt. The route follows the narrow N ridge over a small knoll to the head of Coire Gorm. This ridge is easy angled, but awkward in places. Coire Gorm is an excellent snow-holding gully, and the run down most enjoyable. However, if it is the intention to ascend Meall a' Choire Leith leave the course of the burn at a height of approximately 800m and continue N to reach the col above Coire Liath, from where a stiff ascent leads N to the summit. To include Meall a' Choire Leith adds 2kms and 150m of height, or approximately 45 minutes of skiing to the route.

The route returns via Coire Gorm, but at a height of 620m it is necessary to tear oneself away from the delights of this run to begin the traverse back to the start point. The best line is to ski S to the shielings above the Allt Gleann Da-Eig and then turn W to pass through the low col immediately NE of the start point.

7. Meall Greigh and Meall Garbh

These two Munros are the easiest of the Ben Lawers Group, and to ski both in a day gives a fine ski outing. The terrain is kinder here than on the other Lawers hills. The ridges are broader, and although there are good views across to the cliffs of Ben Lawers, there are no cliffs here. However a degree of competence is still necessary, as both the ascents and descents are steep in places.

The Lawers hamlet on the A827 is a good place to start, from where Lawers Burn can be followed N to shielings and a small dam. The burn has eroded a cosy cutting for itself, and skiing is easier on the open hillside above this. If there is no snow in this lower section a path leads from Machuim and ascends the S bank of the cutting 1km below the dam.

Meall Greigh is the easier of the two mountains. From the shielings by the dam a burn leads to a point just W of the summit. This tends to hold the snow and gives a perfect line of ascent, gentle at first, steepening in the upper section. At a height of about 900m it is necessary to turn E and ascend easily to the summit cairn. The descent of this route gives some fine running with no undue difficulties. There is a good run-out on easy gradients above the shielings.

If continuing from Meall Greigh to Meall Garbh follow the broad and easy ridge W to the col, and then ascend steeply for 200m to gain the broad NE ridge of Meall Garbh, which rises gently to the summit. Meall Garbh is a fine viewpoint.

The descent returns to the col, from where good running over easy grass-based slopes leads back to the dam and shielings.

46. LOCH KENNARD AND LOCH HOIL FOREST CIRCUITS

OS SHEET: 52, 1:25,000 Sheet NN84/94

START POINT: Entrance to forest at S end of Loch na Craige, GR 885451

TOTAL DISTANCE: Loch Kennard Circuit - 7kms, Loch Hoil Circuit - 11kms.

ASCENT: Loch Kennard Circuit - 140m, Loch Hoil Circuit - 150m.

TIME: Loch Kennard Circuit - 2 hours, Loch Hoil Circuit - 3 hours.

TERRAIN: Forest roads, and one short section of forest ride. Steady ascents and descents.

SKIING ABILITIES REQUIRED: Basic skills of ascent and descent.

OTHER ABILITIES REQUIRED: Elementary map reading skills.

SKIING EQUIPMENT NEEDED: Light touring gear.

OTHER EQUIPMENT NEEDED: Lightweight equipment.

SNOW COVER: Will improve as trees grow. Currently this is a young forest - the trees not yet providing conditions for snow accumulation and retention. Tracks well graded requiring minimum cover. High start point at 400m.

APPROACH ROADS: A826 S of Aberfeldy.

Recent planting by private developers has created a vast area of forest to the S of Aberfeldy. At the time of writing the trees are still young - and not tall enough to create the micro-climate of shelter and shade so conducive to snow-holding, as featured in more mature forests. However when the trees do grow this area will have much to offer the skier. Circuits of various lengths can be skied on either side of the A826 from Loch na Craige. There are links to the Craigvinean Forest to the E, itself a vast area of forest with many kilometres of skiable track. The road climbs to 400m above sea level thus giving an accessible high start point. The tracks are good and suitable for those with limited abilities.

Until the trees do grow there are interesting views N across the River Tay to the hills and mountains beyond. Loch Kennard itself is pretty with scattered stances of pines stretching uphill from it. A track running along the N bank allows views from the loch-side

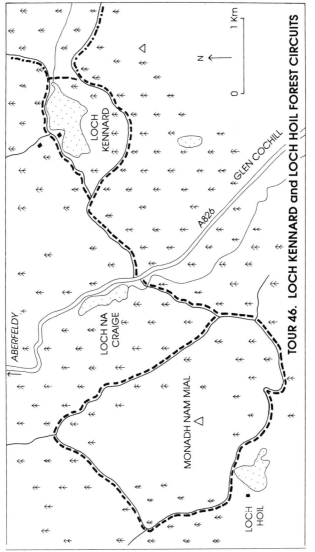

TOUR 46. LOCH KENNARD and LOCH HOIL FOREST CIRCUITS

LOCH KENNARD

GLEN COCHILL

A826

ABERFELDY

LOCH NA CRAIGE

MONADH NAM MIAL

LOCH HOIL

1 Km

N ←

0

across the water to the growing forest beyond.

1. Loch Kennard Circuit

From the S end of Loch na Craige ascend steadily E into the plantation to a junction after 1km. A track descends NE to Loch Kennard, another ascends SE towards Creag a Mhadaidh. These two tracks can be linked by a broad ride which ascends from the E end of the loch, thus allowing a circuit of Loch Kennard. The ride supports a healthy vegetation at present and requires a consolidated snow cover to give good skiing (better ascended than descended).

Tracks from Loch Kennard lead N and E to give much longer circuits, and links with the Craigvinean Forest or N to the Tay Valley E of Aberfeldy (see OS 1:25,000 map).

2. Loch Hoil Circuit

This is not as scenically attractive as the Loch Kennard Circuit and the trees on this side of the road are younger than those planted E of the road. However the tracks are good with more challenging climbs and descents than on the E side. Land-Rover tracks lead SW from the road and circuit the broadly flanked hill, Monadh nam Mial, leaving the plantation briefly (gates) to cross open moor NW of Loch Hoil. There are fine views N to Schiehallion.

47.´ BEN CHONZIE

OS SHEET: 51, (52 if approaching from Loch Turret)

START POINT: Glen Lednock, GR 743272

TOTAL DISTANCE: 12.5kms   ASCENT: 710m   TIME: 4 hours 20 minutes

TERRAIN: Land-Rover track leading to grassy based snow bowls. Slopes steep in places.

SKIING ABILITIES REQUIRED: Ability to ascend steep track and descend broad but steep flanks.

OTHER ABILITIES REQUIRED: Basic/Good winter navigation skills.

SKIING EQUIPMENT NEEDED: Mountain touring gear.

OTHER EQUIPMENT NEEDED: Full mountain equipment.

SNOW COVER: Upper bowls very good and well known for early season potential with skiing in the autumn sometimes possible. Loses snow quickly during thaw.

APPROACH ROADS: A85 to Comrie. Minor road up Glen Lednock.

Ben Chonzie is easily accessible from the Central Scotland population belt and is indeed the nearest mountain of Munro status to both Perth and Edinburgh. The skiing is straightforward mountain skiing with navigational problems reduced by the use of a track for much of the ascent and the existence of fence posts leading to the summit cairn. The grassy terrain means the mountain can be skied after snowfall without any existing snow base. All these factors, combined with the length of time required to complete the tour make Ben Chonzie a popular destination for day trips even in early season when daylight hours are few.

From the minor road in Glen Lednock head N past the buildings at Invergeldie, to gain a broad Land-Rover track. Follow the track N for 1.5kms to a small dam where the track crosses the burn (usually no river crossing problems). Ascend the track E to the head of a broad snow bowl. The track stops short of the head of this bowl. Just before the end of the track and where the gradient becomes decidedly more comfortable ski NNE to gain the fence posts running along the broad and easy S ridge. The fence posts lead to the summit and can be followed. However, the ridge is likely to be blown clear and curves around to the summit. By traversing slightly E of the ridge across Ben Chonzie's SE flank a direct route to the summit takes the skier across the top of a snow-holding bowl.

On a good day the view from the summit is extensive with the Campsie Fells visible to the S and the Glen Shee and Drumochter mountains to the N. Ben Lawers and its subsidiaries dominate in the NW.

Return via the route of ascent, except after leaving the fence and ridge do not head for the track. There is easier, less restricted skiing, along the banks to the N of the burn and along the burn itself. In poor conditions the snow cover is best here.

From Glen Turret

It is possible to ascend Ben Chonzie from Glen Turret via Carn Chois.

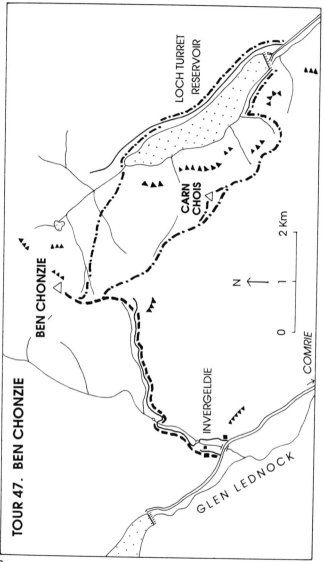

TOUR 47. BEN CHONZIE

A private road serving the Loch Turret Waterworks leads up the glen to a car park at the Glen Turret Reservoir Dam. This is a longer route (16.5kms return from the dam) over the hummocked SE trunk of the mountain. The dam is a high start point (350m above sea level) and any snow which holds in the bowls and depressions around the ridge can be quickly reached.

By close scrutiny of the contours a route on gentle, easy broad slopes can be skied, although the slopes on the E flank of the ridge above the reservoir are steep and craggy. The upper half of the route (between the summit and Carn Chois) along the broad-backed ridge is particularly easy angled and good langlauf terrain. A line of fence posts runs along the ridge, greatly assisting navigation in mist, but not always following the easiest slopes. There are pleasant views descending to the reservoir and S towards Strathearn.

A Land-Rover track along the NE side of the reservoir leads to the rough country at the head of the loch from where a route runs NW to the snow bowls SE of the summit. This gives a lengthy approach to high level snow, and crosses some steep ground.

48. GLEN ARTNEY - UAMH BHEAG

OS SHEET: 57   START POINT: Start of track, GR 713162

TOTAL DISTANCE: 12kms   ASCENT: 639m   TIME: 4 hours

TERRAIN: Grass and heather moorland, with sections of peat hags. Generally easy slopes, but several short steeper sections.

SKIING ABILITIES REQUIRED: Ability to ascend steep slopes, good snowplough, traverse and kick turn - at least.

OTHER ABILITIES REQUIRED: Good winter navigation and hillcraft skills.

SKIING EQUIPMENT NEEDED: General touring gear - mountain touring gear if icy.

OTHER EQUIPMENT NEEDED: Full mountain equipment.

SNOW COVER: Too low to offer guaranteed skiing and the full tour requires snow down to 200m. However N-facing aspect means the upper reaches can be surprisingly good. Depressions in peat retain the snow. Minimum snow cover is needed to ski the moor.

APPROACH ROADS: B827 (Comrie to Braco) and then minor road up Glen Artney. Parking by picnic place - GR 711161.

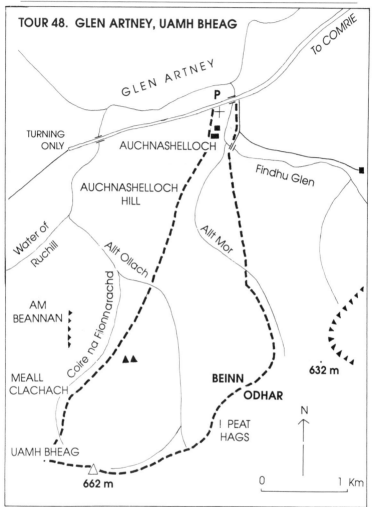

TOUR 48. GLEN ARTNEY, UAMH BHEAG

To COMRIE

GLEN ARTNEY

P

TURNING ONLY

AUCHNASHELLOCH

Findhu Glen

AUCHNASHELLOCH HILL

Water of Ruchill

Allt Ollach

Allt Mor

Coire na Fionnarachd

AM BEANNAN

MEALL CLACHACH

BEINN ODHAR

632 m

UAMH BHEAG

! PEAT HAGS

N

662 m

0   1 Km

A tour off the beaten track, and yet within easy travelling distance from Scotland's main population belt. In fact these two characteristics are the tour's main attractions - the featureless moors themselves being unremarkable. Glen Artney however is charming and the rushing river, picnic place and church handsomely mark the start and end of the tour.

Start E of the church and bridge at a gated track. Follow this half a kilometre S to a junction. The main track continues up Findhu Glen, but fork right and descend on the lower track to a bridge over the burn by a maze of sheep pens. Head due S up broad grass and heather slopes to meet and then follow the course of the Allt Mor to the peaty col E of Beinn Odhar, from which the summit is easily reached. The summit is broad flat and uneventful, but does offer splendid views of Ben Vorlich and Stuc a' Chroin to the NW.

The descent to the col at the head of the broad Allt Ollach Valley is barred by peat groughs, which can make skiing very difficult, but which do at least hold snow in their shady depths. In mist follow the direction of the compass needle, not the enticing peaty hollows.

The valley of the Allt Ollach provides a convenient escape route in bad conditions, however the main route continues W ascending gently and then more steeply to the Ordnance Survey column at height 662m. Fence posts, marking the regional border between Central Region to the S and Tayside Region to the N lead directly to this point, and then to the main summit of Uamh Bheag half a kilometre further W.

The descent follows the course of the Coire na Fionnarachd. Keep to the E bank of the burn, but do not stray too far from its course as the ridge to the E becomes steep and is lined by cliffs further down. The initial half kilometre from Uamh Bheag offers very gentle, easy, confidence boosting slopes, but they do steepen - and become quite testing. When the gradient eases again and the open moor is reached turn NE to the col between the Allt Ollach and the Allt Mor. Traverse around the E flank of Auchnashelloch Hill and descend directly down to the buildings at Auchnashelloch and finally to the gate opposite the entrance to the car park.

49. THE OCHIL HILLS

OS SHEET: 58

The Ochil Hills stretch from Stirling to the Firth of Tay, and are popular, easily accessed hills. The main area of interest to skiers is the highest SW section contained between the A9, the A91 and the A823. Here a number of excursions can be made across superb langlauf terrain of broad slopes and easy gradients. The southern scarp immediately N of the A91 appears steep and imposing, yet by close study of the contours routes of ascent on gradually rising slopes can be found. They lead to a high country of spacious, rounded and flat-topped summits where lengthy routes lie continually above the 500m contour line. This area is renowned for views S across the Forth.

The hills are grassy and skiable with minimum snow cover. However they are not high enough to receive or retain much snow, and they are vulnerable to thawing SW winds. There will be some years when there is very little skiing on The Ochil Hills. They are well located to receive snow from the snow-bearing E winds, in which case W-facing slopes could have the best cover. Otherwise the best snow is on NE-facing slopes. The forest in Glen Sherup holds snow well along its road and rides, and along its upper edge.

The lay of the land makes a ski traverse of the high ground between Glen Devon and Sheriff Muir very attractive. Routes of some 20kms can be skied with 75% of the ground covered above the 500m contour line. From Glen Devon the traverse can be started from Castlehill Reservoir via Glenquey to Whitewisp Hill or from Glen Sherup to Scad Hill and Maddy Moss. From the W the minor road across Sheriff Muir gives a start point at 300m from where the route ascends Mickle Corum and continues to Blairdenon Hill and Ben Buck.

There are a number of circuits possible from the A91 and the A823. The A91 is easily accessible to the population belt to the S, and so probably gives the quickest route to the snow for most. The S scarp of the hills must be climbed but gentle slopes can be sought, and steep slopes at the lower levels where snow is unlikely to be lying anyway can be swiftly ascended on foot. From Alva a track up Silver Glen can be used to reach the broad and grassy SW ridge of Ben Ever, and

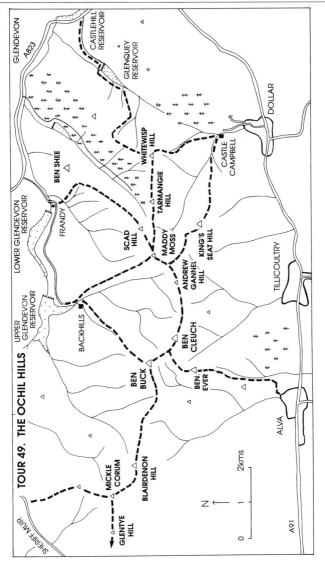

TOUR 49. THE OCHIL HILLS

thence on to Ben Buck, and Ben Cleuch. From Dollar the road to Castle Campbell allows some height to be ascended by vehicle. From the castle a route keeping S of the Burn of Sorrow, ascends W to King's Seat Hill via the easiest slopes of the broad-nosed E ridge. The NE flank of King's Seat Hill holds snow well, but it is steep and requires good technique and confidence in the safeness of the snow, to be skiable. Another route from the castle goes N using the snow-holding slopes of the shallow burn which descends SE from Whitewisp Hill. If joined via Maddy Moss and Tarmangie Hill these two approaches give a worthwhile circuit.

From Glen Devon on the N side there is a choice of routes up easier slopes. A Waterboard road penetrates into the area serving the Upper and Lower Glendevon reservoirs. Locked gates mean access is by foot. From the end of the road at Backhills NE-facing slopes of easy gradient can be climbed to reach the fence posts of Ben Buck. Easy terrain from there via Ben Cleuch and Maddy Moss lead to Skythorn Hill and a gradual descent back to Backhills via the N ridge and the snow-holding slopes above the Broich Burn. Alternatively a descent can be made to Frandy by following the broad ridge trending NE to Scad Hill and Ben Shee, and the tributaries of the Frandy Burn.

The hills above Glen Sherup give some fine skiing (Innerdownie, Whitewisp Hill, Tarmangie Hill, Scad Hill and Ben Shee). The forest holds snow and there are rides leading from the forest road to the open hilltops. Note however that the rides are steep and the forest road does not give good running - particularly in thawing periods when there is a problem of numerous inconvenient burn crossings.

THE CAMPSIE FELLS

The Campsie Fells only enjoy a short season, but when the snow does arrive they are popular with Nordic skiers. This is largely due to close proximity to Glasgow and Stirling. Indeed it is only ten miles as the crow flies from George Square in Glasgow's city centre to the car park on the aptly named "Crow Road", B822, GR 613802. Tours can be snatched in a spare half day or on a moonlit evening after working in Glasgow all day.

The Campsies are well suited to Nordic touring. They are grassy, which gives an ideal base. In some places the tussocky nature of this grass gives uneven, but skiable, terrain. Elsewhere, such as on the approaches to Fin Glen, short grass is skiable with minimum snow cover.

The steep S-facing scarp seen from Glasgow is a misleading facade. Behind lie kilometres of open, undulating moorland, with easy slopes rising to undistinguished high points. The Carron Valley Forest in the N offers many miles of sheltered track skiing, on snow preserving N-facing slopes. One wonders why Glasgow-based skiers travel long distances N for a day's forest skiing when there is snow lying on the more interesting and quieter trails in the Carron Valley Forest. Access to these is from the B818 at either end of the Carron Valley Reservoir.

The Campsies are not high mountains. Earl's Seat, the highest point, is only 578m above sea level. However what is important is that the roads crossing them rise to substantial heights, and give quick access to the snow at upland levels. The B822 Lennoxtown to Fintry road rises to 337m, and is a good start point for tours W towards Earl's Seat or E to Meikle Bin and into the Carron Valley. The minor "Tak ma Doon" road from Kilsyth to Carron Bridge reaches 322m. There are enjoyable routes from this road to Tomtain and Garrel Hill as well as into the forest. Both roads are cleared for vehicle passage eventually by the authorities, but until then may also be closed or difficult to cross in snowy conditions.

Despite close proximity to built-up areas there is an atmosphere of remoteness in the Campsies once Glasgow is out of view, and on a clear day there are interesting views to mountains in the N. Navigation can be difficult in mist, as the moors are quite featureless in places. The scarps and occasional cliffs on their margins should be noted.

There are many skiing routes in the Campsies. In good snow a traverse of the range from the "Tak ma Doon" road to the A875 makes a challenging ski expedition. (Approximately 25kms depending on route.) Forest tracks can be followed from the B818 at either end of the Carron Valley Reservoir to a point just out of the forest NW of Meikle Bin. The N ridge can then be skied to the summit Ordnance Survey triangulation point. This final slope is stepped and steep in places, but the grassy base gives good running for the descent. W of the B822 a short circuit around Dungoil gives another mix of forest and moorland skiing. A track leads W from the road to skirt the N flank of Dungoil before weaving its way S to end by a tributary of the

Clachie Burn. An ascent of Holehead from here can be included before returning to the B822. The forest has a multitude of routes, including the waymarked walkers' trails from the car park and picnic area at the E end of the reservoir.

There has been new forest planting along the NW flank of Lecket Hill, E of the B822. This restricts the skier descending to the road from Lecket Hill. However when the trees grow there may be some very accessible forest skiing here.

Conveniently for the Glasgow-based skier January usually offers the best snow. This means he does not need to travel far to ski at a time of rationed daylight and difficult road conditions.

50. CARRON VALLEY FOREST

OS SHEET: 64, NS 68/78

START POINT: Dam at E end of Carron Valley Reservoir. Parking at side of forest road at S end of dam, GR 718835, or at car park and picnic area, GR 723838.

TOTAL DISTANCE: 11kms   ASCENT: 150m   TIME: 3 hours

TERRAIN: Good forest roads and ride.

SKIING ABILITIES REQUIRED: Mostly easy and suitable for beginners. There is some ascent and descent requiring basic climbing and descending skills - these can be walked.

OTHER ABILITIES REQUIRED: Elementary map reading skills.

SKIING EQUIPMENT NEEDED: Light touring gear.

OTHER EQUIPMENT NEEDED: Lightweight equipment.

SNOW COVER: Dependent on snow lying at 250m. Very short season - January or February being the best months. Some of the roads in the forest likely to have snow cover spoiled by the passage of vehicles - therefore rides or more remote roads are more promising. In places the trees provide excellent shade and help to preserve the snow, but there are many sections which have been felled, or where the trees need to grow more before they will give adequate protection to the snow. If frozen the reservoir has a cooling effect, if however the reservoir is unfrozen and the water still warmer than the forest, the effect will be a warming one.

APPROACH ROADS: B818 Fintry to Carron Bridge. Access to start point from car park and picnic area E of the dam.

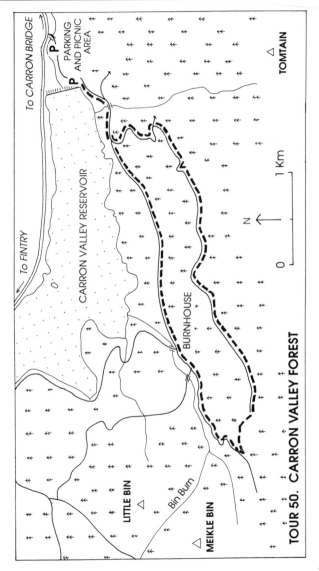

TOUR 50. CARRON VALLEY FOREST

The Carron Valley Forest is a useful skiing area for those living nearby in the Glasgow and Stirling areas. It is a large forest, with several good forest roads and many skiable rides. It is possible to ski all day without skiing any sections twice, or to return several times to explore areas not skied on previous visits. Since the skiing can be easy it is a good place for beginners to try out techniques on sheltered tracks.

The forest does not enjoy the reputation of being scenically inspiring. It faces N and appears dull. This is commercial forest. Do not expect an atmosphere of wilderness. Exploitation by man rules. Vistas over the Carron Valley Reservoir to the sunny S-facing slopes beyond improve an otherwise desperate situation. Some skiers prefer to travel to the Loch Ard and Achray forests in search of more scenic skiing. However, these forests are lower and usually less well blessed with snow than the Carron Valley Forest.

Dirt roads penetrate the forest from both ends of the Carron Valley Reservoir, and skiing can begin at either dam. If transport can be arranged it is possible to follow the forest road along the S side of the reservoir from one dam to the other. This however is a low route dependent on low-lying snow, and likely to have been used by Forestry Commission vehicles. From the dam at the W end of the reservoir it is possible to ascend gradually on good forest roads to a point N of Meikle Bin, from where an assault on the summit can be made. Forest clearance along part of this route has affected its quality, but it gives a long and easy worthwhile descent. There is a maze of good snow-holding rides around Gartcarron Hill, and although not all are skiable, routes to the B822 Lennoxtown/Fintry road give good skiing.

On the NE flank of Little Bin there is a forest road traversing the hill above 250m, which links to roads from the E dam at Burnhouse and the W dam just S of the River Carron. It provides a convenient loop with the track alongside the reservoir. At the moment this upper track runs through land not forested, which means the views across the reservoir and forest are good, but that snow-holding is poor.

There are car parks and picnic areas at the E end of the reservoir and waymarked walkers' routes to choose from. Again a network of rides give interesting explorative skiing.

It is from the E end of the reservoir that the route described here begins. It is an obvious route, since it follows major forest roads. The upper track has particularly favourable snow cover because of its extra height, and since it is not as frequently used by vehicles as the lower road. On a clear day it is possible to see Ben Lomond and other distant hills at certain points along the track.

From the S end of the dam follow the broad forest road SW for almost 1km to a track junction. Turn left (S) and ascend steadily for 0.75km to a fork in the track. The climb will test those still acquiring skills of ascent, but is the price to be paid to reach the skiing on the upper track. Take the right fork and follow this broad forest road W for 3.5kms until it ends. For the most part the skiing is easy, but the track does undulate, with some steady climbing and one short section of fairly steep downhill skiing around a bend. Do not rely on descending to Burnhouse by the routes marked on the 1:50,000 OS maps. The paths shown on the map are not present on the ground.

From the end of the upper track a ride leads off to the right (NW) and traverses the hillside to link with the forest road which ascends from Burnhouse. At the time of writing it is in excellent condition for skiing. It is broad, grassy-based and free of forest litter. The tall trees on either side and the N-facing aspect encourage the snow to linger. If looking for this ride from the W it is 1.5kms from Burnhouse and it runs back at a sharp angle just before the ascending track bends to the right.

The route descends the forest road to Burnhouse. The descent will feel steep to beginners, and is complicated by bends and proximity to the drop down to Bin Burn. Beyond the ruins at Burnhouse follow the track E, running S of the reservoir, which gives easy track skiing back to the start point.

51. LECKET HILL, THE CAMPSIE FELLS

OS SHEET: 64   START POINT: Alnwick Bridge on B822, GR 623807
TOTAL DISTANCE: 7kms   ASCENT: 230m   TIME: 2 hours 10 minutes
TERRAIN: Steep slopes leading to gently undulating tussock grass moorland.
SKIING ABILITIES REQUIRED: Ability to climb and descend steep but broad slopes.
OTHER ABILITIES REQUIRED: Good winter navigation skills.
SKIING EQUIPMENT NEEDED: General touring gear.
OTHER EQUIPMENT NEEDED: Light rucksack.
SNOW COVER: Requires snow at 300m. Prone to rapid thaw.
APPROACH ROADS: B822 Lennoxtown to Fintry. Parking in lay-bys N of bridge at start.

A short tour, offering the Glasgow-based skier a morning or afternoon getting away from it all.

Cross the burn and ascend steeply SSE to Crichton's Cairn (GR 625799) on the ridge above the S-facing scarps of the Campsies. Turn E and follow the ridge over two easy rises to Cort-ma Law. In clear conditions extensive views over the industrial heartlands of Scotland, to the Southern Uplands and even to the fells on Arran can be enjoyed. In bad visibility note the steep and craggy slopes falling away to the S. From Cort-ma Law turn NNW and cross the moor to Lecket Hill. The descent W back to the road and start point begins over gently descending easy terrain. However after 1km steep flanks above the road are encountered. In the past this final descent was not too difficult as the broad slope allowed long traverses in each direction. However new forest planting along the slopes above the B822 have changed the character of this slope. It remains to be seen how the new planting will affect routes to and from Lecket Hill, but it appears that the skier will be restricted to the broad-nosed W ridge of Lecket Hill for out-of-the-forest skiing.

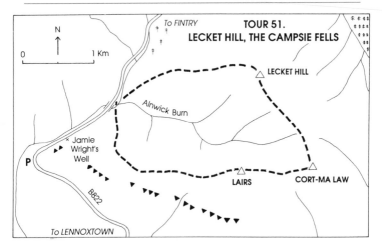

TOUR 51.
LECKET HILL, THE CAMPSIE FELLS

To FINTRY

N

0   1 Km

LECKET HILL

Alnwick Burn

Jamie Wright's Well

P

B822

LAIRS   CORT-MA LAW

To LENNOXTOWN

ALPHABETICAL LIST OF TOURS, ROUTES AND AREAS

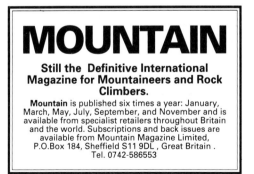

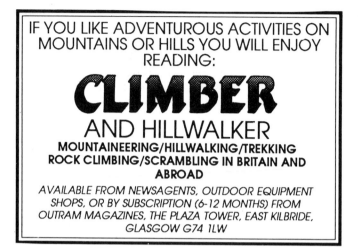

Printed in Gt. Britain by
CARNMOR PRINT & DESIGN
95-97 LONDON RD. PRESTON